# Color
## and
# Crystals

*A Journey Through
the Chakras*

## Other Books by Joy Gardner

*The New Healing Yourself* (The Crossing Press)

*Healing Yourself During Pregnancy* (The Crossing Press)

*The Healing Voice: Traditional & Contemporary Toning,*
*Chanting and Singing* (The Crossing Press)

*The Book of Guidance* (Healing Yourself Press)

# Color
## and
# Crystals

*A Journey Through
the Chakras*

*By Joy Gardner*

The Crossing Press, Freedom, California 95019

## Note to the Reader:

The remedies described herein are given as information, and not as a prescription. They have not been tested on a broad sample of individuals, nor scientifically established. Therefore, neither the author nor the publisher can take responsibility for any ill effects which may be produced as a result of using these remedies: the reader does so at his or her own risk.

Copyright © 1988 by Joy Gardner
Cover illustration by Ivan Marsch
Cover design by Gary Carpenter
Crystal illustrations by Julie Leech
Figure drawings by Peggy McCarty
Circular Chakra drawings by Theresa Mackie and Kelly Van Dolen
Anatomical and other illustrations by Kelly Van Dolen

Printed in the U.S.A.
8th printing 1996

Illustrations from Aleister Crowley's Thoth Tarot Deck reproduced by permission of U.S. Games Systems, Inc. Copyright © 1978, 1983 by U.S. Games Systems, Inc., Stamford, CT 06902, U.S.A. and Samuel Weiser Inc., York Beach, ME 03910, U.S.A. Further reproductions prohibited.

For information on bulk purchases or group discounts for this and other Crossing Press titles, please contact our Special Sales Manager at 800-777-1048.

**Library of Congress Cataloging-in-Publication Data**

Gardner, Joy
    Color and Crystals: a journey through the chakras
1. Chakras. 2. Color—Miscellaneous 3. Crystals—Miscellaneous 4. Healing—Miscellaneous
BF 1999.G28 1988

ISBN 0-89594-5 (pbk.)

# *Contents*

Preface by Swami K.M. Tayumanavar ............................vii

**PART I: INTRODUCTION** ............................................1
Author's Background....................................................9

**PART II: CLEAR QUARTZ CRYSTALS** .................13
Types of Crystals.........................................................18
Crystal Layouts ..........................................................34

**PART III: THE SEVEN CHAKRAS**........................41
Table of Chakras & Stones ..........................................44
First Chakra—Red .....................................................52
Second Chakra—Orange .............................................63
Third Chakra—Yellow.................................................71
Fourth Chakra—Green, Pink ......................................81
Fifth Chakra—Blue.....................................................92
Sixth Chakra—Indigo ...............................................102
Seventh Chakra—Violet .............................................113

**PART IV: INSTRUCTIONS & EXPLANATIONS**   121
Healing With Stones....................................................123
Color Healing..............................................................130
Developing Your Intuition ...........................................139
Mediation and Channeling...........................................142
Toning........................................................................145
The Tarot Archetypes ..................................................147
Seeing Auras..............................................................148
Kundalini ...................................................................150
Karma........................................................................153

Recommended Reading ...............................................154
References...................................................................156
Index..........................................................................157

# Preface

A wise person once defined a fact as "the point at which we have agreed to cease inquiry." *Color and Crystals* owes little to classical research into so called facts and much to personal, intuitive, practical experience. I view this as its strength. Joy Gardner urges us to draw upon our own intuition and to use her book as a guideline, to train and catalyze our minds and spirits rather than imposing yet another set of rigid rules upon us.

Some readers will find conflicting information when comparing this book with other works. This is understandable: even classical sources are not consistent because knowledge of spiritual matters must always pass through subjective experience.

Much of the information in this book has been known and kept secret by the priesthoods since antiquity. This secrecy was appropriate during the dark ages. Now, as humanity moves rapidly toward the light, the opening of the higher chakras is being experienced by increasing numbers of people who have not been initiated into traditional religious orders. *Color and Crystals: A Journey Through the Chakras* translates previously esoteric information into a language that is easily understood. The author appropriately encourages serious students of self realization to find a teacher to serve as a guide through this often uncertain terrain.

There is a great hunger at this time to understand ourselves and our fellow creatures and to commune with the higher spiritual realms. It is appropriate that knowledge of the crystals is coming so rapidly now. The inner teachings of the Eastern priesthoods tell us that crystals appear in the spiritual realms much as they do in the physical world, so they can be used by angelic intelligences to carry vibrations from one plane of existence to another. Likewise, we can use crystals to transmit energy into the higher planes, as we do when we use crystals during meditations for world peace.

This book inspires an invocation of the Kahunas of Hawaii: "Let that which is unknown become known!"

In Love and Light,
Swami K.M. Tayumanavar
Cedarville, California

# PART I

## Introduction

The living body of man and the living body of the earth were constructed in the same way. Through each ran an axis, man's axis being the backbone, the vertebral column, which controlled the equilibrium of his movements and his functions. Along this axis were several vibratory centers wl..ch echoed the primordial sound of life throughout the universe...

*The Book of the Hopi*
by Frank Waters

If you find *Color and Crystals* hard to believe, I can sympathize. When I read *The Secret Life of Plants* by Peter Tompkins, I tried talking to my potted plants, but I just couldn't get into it. After reading *The Spirit of Findhorn* by Eileen Caddy, I wanted to talk to the fairies, but it didn't come naturally to me. Little did I know that within years I'd be carrying on lively conversations with rocks!

As Westerners we believe that life energy is limited to things that move and take nourishment and eliminate waste and reproduce. This is a cultural bias, not shared by most so-called primitive people.

The art of using color, crystals, sound, and the Tarot has existed since ancient times in parts of India, the Orient, Europe, Africa, Hawaii, and among American Indians who have kept the old ways. These people never forgot the inner world of Spirit and how to commune with the plants, animals and rocks.

Western civilization has looked down upon the beliefs of so-called primitive people. But recently there's been a new interest in shamanism, the American Indian practice of living in harmony with nature and working with natural forces.

Suddenly psychologists are studying shamanism and leading vision quests. Meanwhile psychology is moving into the field of metaphysics. Through the exploration of hypnosis and dream therapy, and through the work of Carl Jung, Fritz Perls, Wilhelm Reich, Virginia Satir, Elisabeth Kubler-Ross and others, we're witnessing a remarkable melding of psychology and metaphysics.

The emotions can no longer be separated from the spirit, nor can the emotions or the spirit be divorced from the body. Neither can the body of humanity be separated from the body of the earth. As body, mind and spirit weave together, we find ourselves rediscovering knowledge that's as old as humanity. Foremost among these is the ancient science of the chakras.

3

The chakra system is known to the Hindu yogis and to many other cultures. It's a method of combining philosophy, spirituality, psychology and sexuality in a coherent picture of the whole person. Once this concept is understood, various methods such as color, gemstones, and vibratory sound (toning) can be used to enhance a person's growth or to adjust imbalance.

According to the teachings of the chakras, as our consciousness evolves it follows a predictable path. This can be anticipated by understanding how energy moves up the spine through the chakras. Chakra means wheel or vortex. There are seven major chakras along the spine. Each is a vortex of spinning energy. When a chakra is open, the rate of spin is healthy and the chakra is charged with energy. When a chakra is closed, it doesn't have much energy moving through it.

Each chakra gives off one of the seven colors of the rainbow, so when all the chakras are open and a person is vibrant and healthy, all the colors of the rainbow appear in the electromagnetic energy that surrounds the body, which is that person's aura.

When there's serious physical, emotional or spiritual imbalance, certain colors may be impure, blotchy, muddy, or entirely missing from the aura. These discolorations or omissions (which are visible to one who has inner vision) will eventually lead to physical illness.

Research initiated by the Russians into a technique known as Kirlian photography enables a person to take a picture of the auras. While experimenting with plants, Semyon and Valentina Kirlian found that *before* plants became visibly diseased, there were clear signs of imbalance in their auras. Kirlian photography also gives eivdence of the existence of acupuncture points, which appear as volcanic bursts of white light on the surface of the skin.

For centuries, traditional Chinese acupuncturists have been treating their patients to prevent illness. They have a method of taking pulses for each of the internal organs. They use this information to balance the energy before an imbalance leads to disease. Through treatment at the acupuncture points, they maintain the flow of energy throughout the body by breaking up blockages.

Healing with crystals and gemstones is a similar process. We heal by allowing the aura of the crystal or stone to mix with our own. Through its dominant energy, which is a particular color, it clears and brightens that color in our aura, thus removing blocks, and helping to reestablish balance.

Colored light works in a similar way, with the ray of the light penetrating our aura. This is why the pure colors, such as we find in German glass, are more effective than the blended colors in lower grades of glass and in plastic.

Toning works by penetrating and breaking up blockages through the vibratory energy of sound, a method which closely resembles the effect of acupuncture needles.

4

All illness is characterized by blockage in the channels. We have many channels including acupuncture meridians, nerve channels, arteries and veins. Whenever there's a blockage or injury in one of these channels, it results in inflammation, irritation, and illness.

Color, crystals, and sound are ancient methods of healing. Their vibratory energy breaks up these blockages (whether they're emotional or physical in origin), releasing the energy and allowing it to flow freely.

By knowing which chakras are relatively open and closed, we're better able to understand ourselves. Psychologists and counselors find this information invaluable, both for understanding the inner journeys of their clients, and for having the tools to open and balance the chakras. This book is a melding of metaphysical and psychological insights.

To illustrate how this works, let's follow the progress of one of my clients.

Jack came to see me when his wife left him. He knew he had to make some changes; he'd been depressed, irritable, frustrated, and hard to live with. He was a 45-year-old workaholic, yet his work brought him no real satisfaction. Over the previous eight years, he'd put on weight, started drinking, and was suffering from chronic indigestion.

Jack was a physiotherapist. His father was a doctor, a busy man who rarely had time for his large family. Jack learned early in life that he could win his father's attention through his interest in medicine.

Jack is an example of an imbalanced third chakra personality. When consciousness evolves to the third chakra, there's a need to find our unique gift and express it. We do this naturally when our parents encourage us to explore our world and discover who we are. But this rarely happens.

Jack needed to rebuild on a firm foundation (first chakra). To do this, he needed to go back into childhood and take down the old unhealthy foundation by clearing out unfinished business and releasing old emotions. I used light hypnosis to help Jack explore his childhood. I put a small crystal ball on the pillow above his head where it touched his crown chakra, to help him remember his past. Then I asked him to go back to a particular incident when he desperately wanted his father's love and approval.

Jack found himself as a young boy at a piano recital. He wasn't nervous; he was confident and excited about playing for an audience. He was evidently a highly talented young musician, and his concert was a great success, except for the glaring absence of his father.

"How can he be so cold, so blind?" Tears gathered in the corners of Jack's eyes.

I touched his arm gently. "Could you, the grown-up Jack, pretend you're a friend of the family and go up to the boy and give him a hug and tell him he was wonderful?"

5

Jack nodded. I placed a pillow against his chest, and he hugged that pillow against his heart and cried and cried.

After awhile I asked, "How did the boy respond?"

Jack nodded appreciatively, a big smile on his face.

I suggested that he visualize the child becoming very small and make a place for him in his heart so that neither of them would have to be alone again. Then I placed a rose quartz over his heart to heal the old pain.

When we finished the session, Jack's face was radiant. I urged him to wear a citrine pendant. The citrine is a yellow crystal (the color for the third chakra). It helps a person get in touch with his or her personal power. It's also a potent stone for overcoming addictions and strengthening will power. I gave him a piece of rose quartz and asked him to keep it with him to overcome the need for alcohol. And I recommended that he wear a turquoise belt buckle or ring to aid his digestion and give him a sense of balance and self-confidence.

When he returned two weeks later, he had lost weight, stopped drinking alcohol (though he still drank coffee and smoked cigarettes) and had overcome his digestive problems.

Shortly after, he quit his job and started working in a band with his synthesizer. He never did get back together with his wife, but they were able to resolve their hostilities and became good friends.

Now that you've seen how the chakra system can work on an individual (the microcosm), let's look at how it works on the world (the macrocosm). According to Sri Yukteswar, an East Indian Swami and guru of Yogananda (author of *Autobiography of a Yogi*), we live currently in what is known in Hindu philosophy as the Dwapara Yuga. Yugas are 1200 year segments of a 24,000 year cycle, the time it takes (according to Oriental astronomy) for our sun to revolve around another star (its dual). In the course of the sun's cycle, it also revolves around a grand center called Brahma, the seat of universal magnetism, which influences human awareness.

When our sun is closest to Brahma, humans are capable of comprehending All That Is. This time period is called Satya Yuga. Its influence lasts for 4800 years. If we look at it in terms of human development as we know it, we can imagine a golden age of human awareness occurring during the civilization of Atlantis.

Edgar Cayce and Ruth Montgomery, both reputable psychics, describe a time of high civilization in early Atlantis, when the earth was peopled by Light Beings who did not require food and were able to dematerialize and appear at several places at once. The Atlanteans were well known for their extensive use of crystals for practical and spiritual purposes. These early humans as beings who lived primarily through the energies of the seventh and sixth chakras.

6

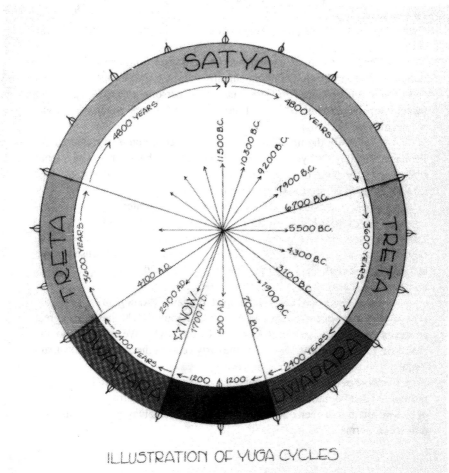

ILLUSTRATION OF YUGA CYCLES

Sri Yukteswar states that the center of the Satya Yuga was 11,501 B.C. Edgar Cayce gives 12,000 B.C. as the date when Atlantis sank into the sea. Enlightened Atlanteans who foresaw the fall of Atlantis and the flood built huge ships and migrated to Egypt (and elsewhere), where they were received as Sons of God. They brought the gifts of astronomy, mathematics, music, architecture and medicine to the Egyptians. In fact, the Tibetan, Mayan, Hebrew, Celtic, Hawaiian Kahuna, and Hindu cultures are all believed to have similar origins.

Gradually human intelligence and intuition diminished, and most humans lost the ability to commune directly with All That Is. We entered the Treta Yuga, which lasted for 3600 years. The personalities that typify this period correspond to the fifth and fourth chakras (in their balanced and unbalanced manifestations).

Eventually the imbalance became more common as we entered the Dwapara Yuga, a 2400 year period. I see this era as characterized by people who lived primarily through their third chakra, cut off from spiritual knowledge and obsessed with intellect and power.

Finally the cycle reached its lowest ebb as we entered the Kali Yuga, a period which lasted 2400 years (1200 descending and 1200 ascending). During this time, normal human awareness could not comprehend anything beyond physical reality, which typifies human consciousness focused in the second and first chakras. This is the time we think of as the era of the cave men and the Dark Ages.

From that point we evolved upward again. The beginning of the ascent of Kali Yuga occurred around A.D. 500. Around 1600 there were great advances in science and improvements in life style. We moved into the Dwapara Yuga in 1700. We are still in the early years of the ascending Dwapara Yuga.

Most people in the present era live primarily in their first two chakras and are just beginning to develop their third. It's not surprising that those of us who attempt to open our higher chakras find ourselves going against current social norms.

•

I hope you'll enjoy this journey through the chakras. It will work on the microcosmic and the macrocosmic levels. It will help you to understand the evolution and devolution of human awareness—in history, in the individual and in yourself. When you truly understand the chakra system, you'll possess the most wonderful tool for understanding All That Is.

# Author's Background

I've been working as a wholistic counselor, teacher, and author since 1972. As a counselor I see individuals, couples and children for a wide range of emotional and physical problems. I deal with death and loss and emotional release. I facilitate past life regressions, hypnotherapy, visualization, and finding the underlying emotional and spiritual cause of physical illness.

I decided in the third grade that I would be a writer. When I was in high school, I remember reading Carl Jung and thinking that my mission in life would be to bring together concepts of the East and West.

My mother is an intuitive woman, and by her example she taught me to trust my intuition. On several occasions when I was a child, my mother would have dreams in which someone she knew had died. The next day we'd receive a call telling us that the person in her dream was dead.

I also inherited my mother's extreme love of nature. As a child in Poland she spent time with the gypsies, drawn to their beautiful music, and she learned to tell fortunes with cards and to read palms. I remember her dressing up like a gypsy fortune teller and setting up a tent at a fund-raising affair when I was about eight years old. That was the last time she told fortunes. She was too good at it; it disturbed her to know when terrible things were going to happen to people.

My older brother was another strong influence. He was five years older than me. Don introduced me to existentialism and Zen Buddhism. At the age of thirteen, I was meditating in front of a big black Buddha, burning incense in my bedroom.

In 1970 I made my entry into the healing arts by becoming an herbalist. In 1972 I wrote *Healing Yourself*, a book about home remedies that has evolved through seven editions and sold over 100,000 copies. Gradually I expanded into acupuncture and Bach Flower Remedies. I was meditating regularly, and during my meditations it was not uncommon for me to get messages. I would often receive excellent advice about my day-to-day affairs and my personal problems. I learned to trust this inner voice, though I didn't tell other people about it until many years later, after I read Eileen Caddy's books about Findhorn. She, too, heard an inner voice, giving her messages which she called guidance.

In 1974 I received a series of spiritual journeys from Rev. Helena Ram, a psychic in Seattle. These are guided visualizations in which a person walks along their life path. It is like a waking dream in which you experience and interpret the images that your subconscious brings up. During these journeys I opened to the spiritual world within and met two of my spirit guides. Later I studied with Helena Ram and learned to use light hypnosis to guide people through spiritual journeys, to help them find their spirit guides, and to go into past lives.

Over the next several years I was in gestalt, Jungian and bioenergetic therapies. Then I studied gestalt with Bethal Phaigh and death and loss work with Elisabeth Kubler-Ross.

In 1977 I began channeling Dr. Laing, a spirit guide and kind entity who visited me for about an hour at a time, usually when I was driving long distances. He gave me long and fascinating lectures about various aspects of metaphysical healing. My other spirit guides had not been nearly so articulate.

Within a short time, the main focus of his lectures turned to the use of color for healing and inner growth. He organized these lectures around the chakras, beginning with the first (at the tailbone) and moving upward. At that time, I knew a little about the chakras but I hadn't even heard of color healing and I was quite skeptical. Later I began to read about color in the few books that were then available, and I was delighted to find that Dr. Laing's information was consistent with what I was reading.

Under Laing's instruction I began teaching workshops on color. Then I was introduced to *The Spiritual Value of Gemstones*, channeled by Lenora Huett, and found it inspiring. I began to incorporate the stones into the workshop that was then called Color, Sound, and Gemstones. The information covered was so complex that I prepared an outline for my students so that they wouldn't have to take too many notes. Over the next eight years that outline grew into a booklet and then into a full-sized book, which is now *Color and Crystals*.

In the beginning, my work with the stones was mostly intellectual. Then I received a crystal balancing and toning from a wonderful woman who was an opera singer. It was a remarkable experience. It felt as though my third eye was being drilled open. The woman who gave me this gift said, "This work will come naturally to you, because you did it in a past life." I never saw her again. I don't even remember her name.

I found myself placing stones on almost all my clients. I was astonished by how powerful the stones were. I was doing the same counseling work, but it was going from two to twenty times faster. Whether I was doing a past life regression or hypnosis or channeling or working on emotional release, everything was easier.

Around that time, I discovered Katrina Raphaell's wonderful books, *Crystal Enlightenment* and *Crystal Healing*, which opened up whole new dimensions. Then Dr. Laing began channeling specific information about different kinds of clear quartz crystals, and the stones themselves began to give me information.

I also use toning in my work. After I received the crystal balancing and toning treatment, I lost my inhibition about using my voice and felt free to make whatever sounds came through. These sounds became an important part of the healing process.

I'm not a trance channel. When Dr. Laing speaks I'm fully awake and conscious. I hear his lectures as if they were my own thoughts, but they have a different quality. It could be argued that Dr. Laing is just an aspect of myself. Indeed, it could be argued that everyone who has ever lived and every spirit both incarnate and discarnate is also an aspect of myself. In fact I am quite convinced that the Great Spirit is an aspect of myself and vice versa. But we must make distinctions—I experience Dr. Laing as an entity quite separate from myself.

Dr. Laing was born before the turn of the century in India. His father was a British doctor, and both parents were mystics. Laing returned to England and became a doctor himself. Eventually he died in London. He is not to be confused with Dr. William Lang, a guide who worked through George Chapman in England. Nor should he be confused with R.D. Laing, a contemporary psychologist.

There are other guides who have been a great help, including Emily who originally came to me when I channeled her for one of my clients (something I rarely do, since I prefer to help people to channel their own guides). Emily has a wonderful gift for working with stones, and she continues to be a great help to me.

I'm also indebted to Pink Tara, a newly emerged sister-aspect of the **Hindu deity, Green Tara, Pink Tara appeared simultaneously to myself and** several other women (without prior communication between us) during the past year. She embodies gentle strength. She is the Guardian of color and of the arts. Pink Tara has guided me in the use of the pink and green stones for the heart chakra.

I wish to give thanks directly to the Rock Kingdom, for allowing me to enter into direct communion with their consciousness and to bring this knowledge into written form.

I'm also grateful to my clients, particularly those who were receptive to my early experiments. Their faith in me and their feedback on the effects of the stones have been invaluable. Much of the knowledge I've gained has come while working with my clients.

In 1985 I channeled *The Book of Guidance* which brings knowledge of the spirit world (including information about color) into direct and practical application on the earth plane. I refer repeatedly to this earlier work in *Color and Crystals.*

I don't pretend to have much expertise in metaphysics. Whenever confronted with a book on this topic, I jump in and try the techniques rather

11

than delving into the theory. It is my limited knowledge which prompted me to write this book. Those who are steeped in metaphysics, like experts in any field, become so adept at speaking their specialized language that they often forget how to translate it for ordinary people. Because I remember how it feels to try to weave my way through areas that often seem incomprehensible, I hope to act as a bridge, providing tools to make this task easier for the reader.

Neither am I a mineralogist. Though I understand the stones on a spiritual level, I make no pretense at having a scientific mastery of the subject.

In each aspect of its evolution, *Color and Crystals* has reflected my own evolution. It began as a roadmap for my understanding as I struggled to bring the concept of the chakras into a context that was meaningful to me. That was a third chakra, intellectual experience.

During that time in my life I studied gestalt with Bethal Phaigh and death and loss with Elisabeth Kubler-Ross, which gave me ample opportunity to release the emotions that had been closing off my heart chakra. That gave me many insights into the fourth chakra.

My fifth chakra opened considerably when I received initiation into Reichi (a method of healing with the hands, and distant healing). I channeled more information from Dr. Laing and later *The Book of Guidance*.

I continued to follow the guidance that I received from my meditations, my dreams, and my spirit guides. Then I reached the point where I needed to find a flesh and blood person who had experienced self realization. I needed to talk to someone about my own inner struggle. It was no longer adequate to read books, no matter how enlightened the writers.

I met Swami Tayumanavar (Swami Ty) at the Evergreen Retreat in Idaho where we were both teaching, and we became fast friends. I noticed that when I stood alongside him my energy soared to my higher chakras. Over the next few months, I saw that my friend embodied the virtues that I was seeking. It was a great relief to find someone who knew his path and could give me support as I moved along mine. Finally the awareness that I longed for began to unfold, and I was able to understand and write about the sixth and seventh chakras.

I also want to thank my editor, Elaine Gill, for her continuing support, and my publishers, John and Elaine Gill. for their personal integrity, that goes far beyond a business relationship.

The process is perpetually unfolding. I offer this book in a spirit of sharing.

Joy Gardner

# PART II

---

## Clear Quartz Crystals

Why have crystals suddenly become so popular? The clear quartz crystal holds the vibration of White Light, and as we open our higher chakras we become receptive to that Light and to the crystals that embody it.

The crystals have been there all along, but we were blind to their beauty. Since they were so abundant, we didn't consider them precious. Similarly, the Light of Spirit has been there all along, but we've been blind to it because we didn't love ourselves. Now that we're moving toward the Light, the crystals are ready to reflect back the light that we're finding within. The infinite variety of crystals assures us that we can be totally unique and remain beautifully in the Light.

When we meditate with crystals or use them for healing, they energize our chakras. They burn through our blocks and help to dispel our darkness.

As Chrysta Faye Burka describes in her wonderful book, *Clearing Crystal Consciousness*, the crystal is a metaphor for our own growth from unconsciousness to consciousness. It forms a perfect point, reflecting our growth toward awareness and enlightenment.

Katrina Rafaell says that the six sides of the crystal symbolize the six chakras, with the termination at the crown connecting with the infinite. Many crystals are milky at the base, gaining greater clarity as they reach the terminated peak, just as our dullness of consciousness clears as we grow closer to union with our infinite selves. Then we're better able to reflect the clear white light as we *become* that light in a physical form.

Burka says that like the crystal we're constantly channeling and clearing energy by clearing out our emotional pain. As our energy becomes clear, we become a pure channel for universal life energy. She says that the function of crystals is to maintain the balance of the electro-magnetic field: the balance between the electrical energies surrounding the earth and the magnetic energies between the poles. This same spiralling electrical field and magnetic polarity exist within each atom and each subatomic particle, within each cell and each organ, within each living and non-living thing, and within the human aura.

In the body at a cellular level, this balance is maintained by silica, which has the exact chemical composition as of natural quartz crystal. Hence, the human body is like liquid crystal. This helps to explain why the crystals have such great power to affect our bodies and our souls.

"As your energy becomes clear," says Burka, "you become a pure channel for universal life energy. You become your own crystal as you integrate and connect directly with your spiritual dimension."

In fact, I've found that I don't need crystals. Everything I do with crystals, I can do without them. But crystals make it easier.

One of my guides says that during meditation, the silica particles in our heads become magnetically charged and align themselves around the pituitary and pineal glands, which stimulates those glands. This helps to explain both the feelings of well-being and the experience of White Light or Enlightenment which sometimes accompany deep meditation.

Clear quartz crystals contain the full spectrum of the energy of the seven rays. They bring more color and light into the human aura. They heal the body indirectly, by filling in the missing colors in the aura. Rafaell says that they vibrate the aura at such a rate that they dissipate the dark shadows that cloud the aura. This helps to explain why clear quartz crystals can balance energy and heal at all levels, including the emotional, spiritual, and physical— provided that we're willing to release old pains and take on new energy.

Crystals act like radio transmitters. They have the power to transmit and amplify our energies, good or bad. They're neutral in themselves, but they can be charged with whatever energy we put into them, and they can transmit this energy into the atmosphere, into another person's aura, or thoughts, or energy body.

Since crystals have the power to penetrate the human aura, be very careful about who you allow to treat you. Never open yourself to a treatment unless you feel entirely comfortable with the energy of the person giving the treatment.

Remember that your energy is being affected if you're in the vicinity of a crystal, whether you're the healer, or the client. It's a process that involves both people, and while you may be doing a healing for someone else, if you're open to it, you may find that you're also being healed. On the other hand, if you're overly attached to your role as healer, you may find that this work will drain you.

The uses for crystals are endless. There are personal crystals that you hold when you meditate and there are crystals that you use for healing. Crystals may be placed around your house, for their great beauty and because they give off negative ions, which create a sense of well-being .

Some people say that chipped crystals should not be used for healing. Yet some of my favorite crystals have small chips, and they are powerful healers. However, if the chips actually change the shape of a stone, this may interfere with its effectiveness. For example, a channeling crystal should have a seven-sided face. If the chip destroys one of the seven sides (so that it's difficult to tell whether it actually is seven-sided), this is likely to weaken the channeling effect of the crystal.

Some chips interfere with the energy flow of the crystal, whereas others do not. If you are strongly drawn to a particular crystal, then you are in harmony with its energy, and you don't have to worry about whether it is chipped or not. We all carry around chips of one kind or another.

When you're at someone else's home and looking through their crystals, you can tell a great deal about them by observing the types of stones they've attracted into their lives. For example, I was visiting the home of a woman who lived in an elegant mansion. On the table I saw a crystal that had a large baby within. As I explain (see Index) this kind of crystal is useful for manifestation, so it helps you to achieve the kind of physical surroundings you desire. Such crystals are difficult to find. This woman knew nothing about babies within, but she was intuitively attracted to this crystal.

# Types of Crystals

You may use the following guidelines to select crystals that will be appropriate for your needs. This information was received mostly from Dr. Laing and combined with other sources.

There are various types of clear quartz crystals.

## Single Terminated

This is the most common kind of crystal, with a single six-sided point at one end, which is why it's also called a point.

Single terminated crystals are used to charge the chakras, or to disperse negative energy. When using single terminated crystals for healing, bring in energy by pointing them inward—for example, toward a large stone at the

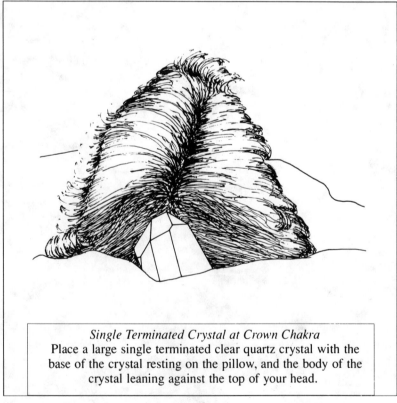

*Single Terminated Crystal at Crown Chakra*
Place a large single terminated clear quartz crystal with the base of the crystal resting on the pillow, and the body of the crystal leaning against the top of your head.

center of a particular chakra. Point them outward (away from the stone at the center of a chakra) to disperse energy, or for cleansing. To open or enhance the energy at your crown chakra, place a large single terminated clear quartz crystal with the base resting on the pillow, and the body of the crystal leaning against the top of your head. This will help you to open to the White Light of Spirit.

Single terminated crystals are often used for jewelry. Be cautious about wearing crystals, because they absorb energy like a sponge. If you're in a bad mood, your crystal will hold that energy and reflect it back to you. If you're around negative people, it will take on their negativity.

Your crystal will be less vulnerable to other people's energy if you wear it inside your shirt, where it's next to your skin and shielded by your clothing. Some people like to wear their crystal in a little bag around their neck. This protects the crystal from other people's energy, but it's less effective for you than wearing it next to your skin.

On the other hand, if you're feeling good and you're around other people who are feeling good, wear your crystal visibly so it can absorb that energy and reflect it back to you. It's excellent to wear crystals for ceremonial purposes or before ceremonies to cleanse your energy and brighten your aura. If you're not feeling well, the crystal will draw off some of your negativity and will charge your aura with light. When it does this, we say that the crystal is working hard. When it works too hard it becomes exhausted. Then it's no longer strong enough to absorb negativity nor to charge your energy, it's likely to send back negativity. That's why we cleanse the crystals.

## Double Terminated

Double terminated usually describes crystals that have one point at each opposite end. Double terminated crystals may grow in soft clay, or they may grow as part of a crystal cluster. Be wary of crystals that have been cut to look as if they are double terminated; unless the person who cut the stone is highly conscious, the effect is not comparable to that of true double terminated crystals.

I use double terminated crystals to open a line of energy between two or more chakras. For example, I was treating a woman who complained of being depressed. She was a workaholic who had virtually no energy at her second chakra and an overabundance of energy at her third chakra. At the age of 45, she was feeling the loss of not having had children.

I did a layout of stones at her second chakra and put one stone at her third chakra. Then I put the double terminated crystal between the second and third chakras. During the session, she grieved over the baby she never had, and reached a level of acceptance about that loss. When I felt her chakras later, the

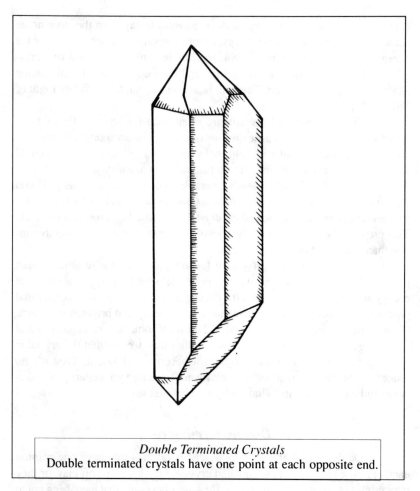

**Double Terminated Crystals**
Double terminated crystals have one point at each opposite end.

energy had increased at the second chakra and leveled out at her third. She felt much better.

Double terminated can also describe crystals that have a single (or multiple) point at one end, and multiple points at the opposite end. I use double terminated and multi-terminated crystals interchangeably. If a crystal has a large termination at one end and many small terminations at the other, I consider the one termination its main end. In doing layouts I will put the main end toward the head.

### Barnacle Crystals

Sometimes you'll find a whole side of a crystal covered with small crystals, like barnacles. Then you'll know that the larger crystal is like an old

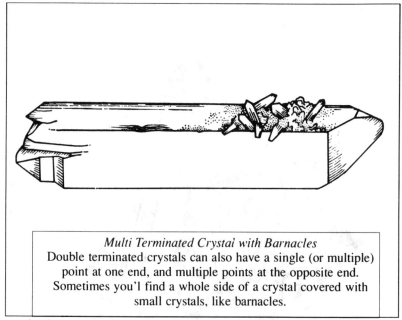

*Multi Terminated Crystal with Barnacles*
Double terminated crystals can also have a single (or multiple)
point at one end, and multiple points at the opposite end.
Sometimes you'l find a whole side of a crystal covered with
small crystals, like barnacles.

matriarch or patriarch who is well loved by the clan and whose wisdom can
be trusted. Hold the barnacle crystal while you meditate and it will give you
insights that will help you to deal with family or community problems. This
crystal makes a wonderful companion, especially if you feel the loss of a
beloved grandparent or a wise old family member.

## Crystal Clusters

Clusters of crystals are formed when silica cools rapidly, causing
many terminations to jut out, often in multiple directions. The individual crystals reflect light and energy back and forth to one another, creating a strong
healing and cleansing vibration. These crystals can be used to clear the energy in a room. They are self-cleansing to some extent because they charge each
other, but be sure to cleanse them periodically, especially if they've been exposed to a lot of negativity. They can also be used to cleanse other stones, which
can be placed upon them. A crystal cluster makes an excellent pedestal for a
crystal ball.

Clusters are good for diversified people who shoot off in many different directions. Just contemplate the cluster and it will help you to feel better about yourself.

The crystal cluster is a perfect group crystal. The cluster is a group of
unique and beautiful individuals joined at the stone matrix from which they all
emerge. If you belong to a group that has a higher purpose, try to find a crys-

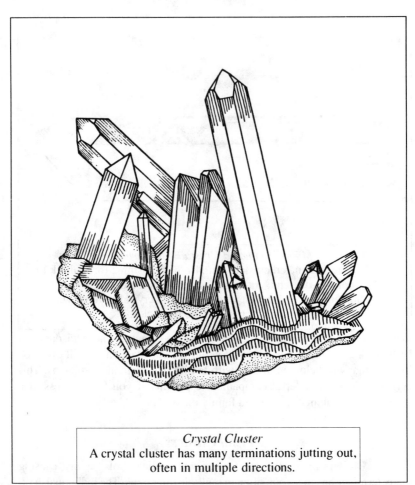

*Crystal Cluster*
A crystal cluster has many terminations jutting out,
often in multiple directions.

tal cluster that reflects the perfection of your group. Place it at the center of the room, or at the center of your meditation circle whenever you gather. If everyone in the group feels attuned to the crystal cluster, it will strengthen your group and help it to find a solid base and to perfect itself—especially if it is verbalized that this is the reason for the placement of the crystal.

## Herkimer Diamonds

These are not diamonds, but small crystals with diamond-like clarity, mined only in Herkimer County, New York. Their double terminated bodies tend to be relatively short and close in size to the terminations. They have a higher hardness factor than any other quartz (7.5 instead of 7). Since the

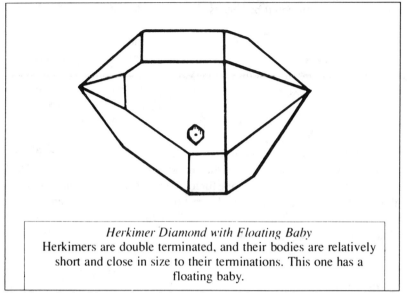

*Herkimer Diamond with Floating Baby*
Herkimers are double terminated, and their bodies are relatively
short and close in size to their terminations. This one has a
floating baby.

Herkimer is double terminated, it can be used for anything that a double terminated crystal is used for.

In *The Crystal Connection*, Vicki and Randall Baer explain that the
characteristics of the Herkimer give it very high frequency capacities and a
versatile energy formulation range. I have a large Herkimer which I use like a
laser, in conjunction with very high-pitched tone, to cut through blockages and
to break up concentrations of energy.

When I feel this treatment is needed, I ask permission from my client
("I want to make an intense, high-pitched sound. Is that all right?"), then I'll
aim one of the terminations toward the area that's blocked and tone, usually
making the ee sound at a very high pitch. The shock value of the tone (even
with the warning), in combination with the high frequency intensification of
the Herkimer, creates a dramatic and powerful effect that causes a person to
instantly drop whatever it was that they were holding onto, and the blockage
dissolves. A similar effect can be created with a toning crystal, as described
below.

The Herkimer can help you to remember and to work through your
dreams. Place one inside your pillowcase so it will be near your head at night.

The Herkimer has a happy, bubbly kind of energy.

Hold it when you meditate or wear it or keep it in your shirt pocket
for a few days if you're feeling depressed. It can quickly change your energies. But don't wear it on a regular basis because over a period of months, it
can alter your energies so radically that you may become extremely nervous

and disoriented. This could be because it puts you too much into the dream world.

Long narrow crystals intensify the length and breadth of your sound vibrations while toning or singing. They're either single or double terminated. If they're double terminated, they usually have just one termination at each end. Randall and Vicki Baer write that "the longer the body and the greater the clarity and mass, the greater the amplification. A longer body also allows for a higher degree of versatile energy input and modulation potential."

When selecting a crystal for toning, try toning with it to see if you can hold the tones for longer, and if the vibratory sound is more forceful. Not every long narrow crystal is effective for toning, and some are far more powerful than others (not necessarily the longest ones). These crystals can also be used like wands for crystal balancing. The light energy of these long crystals helps to create the sensitivity that is required to feel the spin in someone else's chakras.

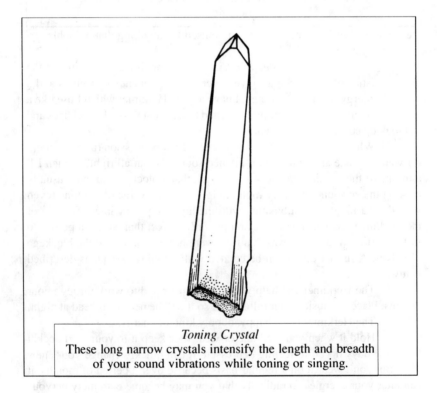

*Toning Crystal*
These long narrow crystals intensify the length and breadth of your sound vibrations while toning or singing.

## Clear Crystals

Crystals that are as clear as glass (even if they contain veils or fractures or other patterns) have the energy of clarity and will help you to expand your consciousness. They will clear your head, enhance your receptivity to guidance, and facilitate visualization. A clear crystal can be placed at the third eye while lying down. Or you can hold it during meditation and, if you like, you can gaze into it or place it on top of your head for greater clarity.

## Long Thin Delicate Crystals

Small delicate crystals enhance whatever work is being done. When faced inward for charging, they introduce a small jolt of energy. When faced outward for cleansing, they create a subtle passageway for unwanted energy to escape. They're virtually indispensable for doing layouts on the sixth chakra, where there isn't enough space to use larger crystals—particularly on people with narrow foreheads.

## Rainbows

Most crystals will reflect colored light when held to the sun, but rainbow crystals have special formations that reflect exquisite colorful patterns. These are happiness crystals. When you meditate with them and inhale their colors into your heart, they'll bring you comfort and joy.

## Veils

These are rainbow crystals in which the colors are reflected off a veil-like surface within the crystal. Depending on the light or the angle at which you hold it, this formation sometimes appears as silver, and sometimes as a thin dark veil. These are mysterious crystals. The darkness will help you to understand your own darkness (negativity, fear, anger) and transform it into light.

The formations that cause veils are fractures that occur as a result of trauma to the crystal, such as being dropped or jostled severely. The crystal's ability to transform this trauma into a thing of beauty is like the human experience of having a severe emotional ailment, or perhaps a life-threatening disease, that is transformed into an opportunity for personal and spiritual growth. When you have mastered your own darkness, you will have the power to heal others. You can draw out their negativity, fear, and anger, and help them to transform it.

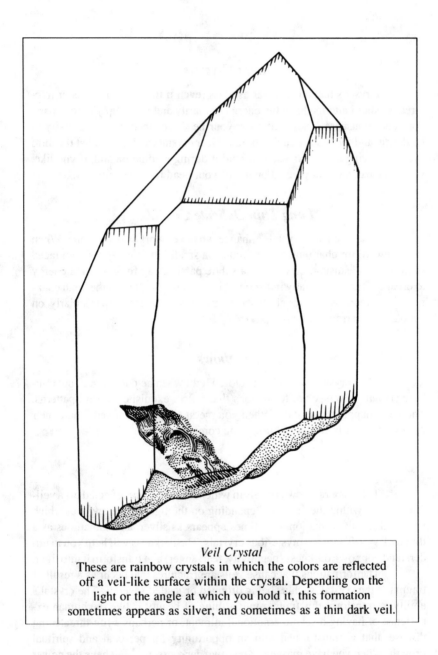

*Veil Crystal*
These are rainbow crystals in which the colors are reflected
off a veil-like surface within the crystal. Depending on the
light or the angle at which you hold it, this formation
sometimes appears as silver, and sometimes as a thin dark veil.

## Craters

Sometimes you'll see a hole in a crystal that looks like a crater. When
that hole is in the perfect shape of an inverse crystal, it's an indication that a

smaller crystal once made its home there. These crater crystals are a metaphor for motherhood at its best. The larger crystal possessed the ability to yield gracefully, allowing the baby crystal to live within its flesh. And then, when the ripening was complete, it allowed the smaller crystal to pop out, fully formed. So this crater crystal combines the qualities of yielding, nurturing, and letting go. When you hold these crystals and meditate with them, they will help you to develop these qualities within yourself.

These crystals are good for parents, teachers, and people who have to be self-sacrificing. Ultimately, it teaches you to turn your pain into pearls. It reminds you that when you explore the bottom of the pit, you'll come out the other side. Just as every mountain has a valley, so does every valley have two mountains. There is great depth to these crystals. Particularly when the imprint is distinct, they enable you to go inward and bring things to the surface that have been buried.

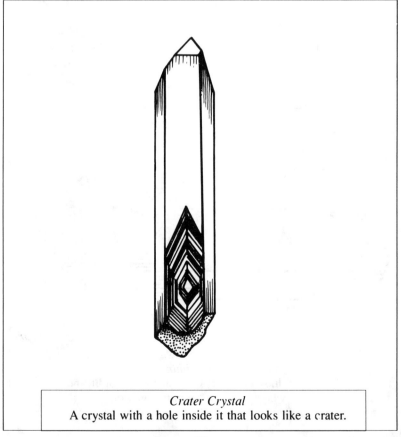

*Crater Crystal*
A crystal with a hole inside it that looks like a crater.

## Baby Within

When you gaze into a clear quartz crystal, you may find a whole baby crystal in the interior. Usually they grow from the sides of the crystal, but I've even seen them growing out of a veil within the crystal, or seeming to float in space within the crystal. Crystals that have a baby within are valuable for manifestation.

If there's something you want to manifest (to create), begin by asking yourself, "Is this *really* something I want? Is there any reason why I might not want it?" If a part of you wants something and another part doesn't, you'll be working against yourself, so it's important to begin by acknowledging and then clearing away any feelings of ambivalence.

When you've done this, you can meditate with this crystal, concentrate on your first chakra, visualize what you want and bring it consciously into a concrete thought form. Feel that thought becoming dense as it turns into reality.

These crystals can be used in a similar manner to increase fertility. This can refer to babies, but it can also relate to artistic creativity, farming, and creative thinking. However, be cautious about birth control if you're using this crystal and you don't want to create a baby.

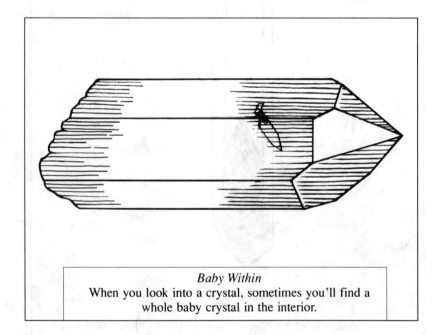

*Baby Within*
When you look into a crystal, sometimes you'll find a
whole baby crystal in the interior.

## In and Out Crystal

When you have a clear quartz crystal that has a small crystal within protruding through to the outside, you've found a very special gift. These in and out crystals help bridge the gap between the inner and outer worlds. If you're getting in touch with your inner self and want support in expressing what you're experiencing, this crystal will help you. If you're stuck in events of the past, this crystal will help bring you into the present.

This crystal is invaluable for people who are moving into their higher chakras and attempting to share this knowledge with others. It's also ideal for public speakers lecturing on metaphysical topics, especially if they're breaking new ground. For example, I met a chiropractor who was studying crystal healing from a scientific viewpoint. He intended to give classes on crystal healing to doctors. I wanted to encourage him in this direction, so I gave him an in and out crystal.

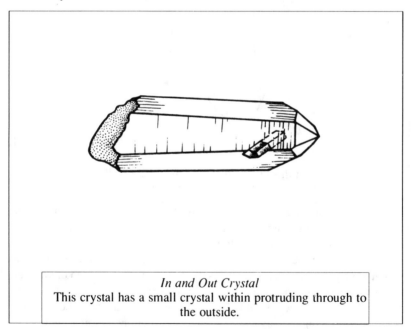

*In and Out Crystal*
This crystal has a small crystal within protruding through to the outside.

## Wall Crystal

When you look within a crystal and there seems to be a wall—an inner facet dividing the crystal—this stone can bring understanding in divisive situations. If you find yourself locked in an intense argument, back off and take the

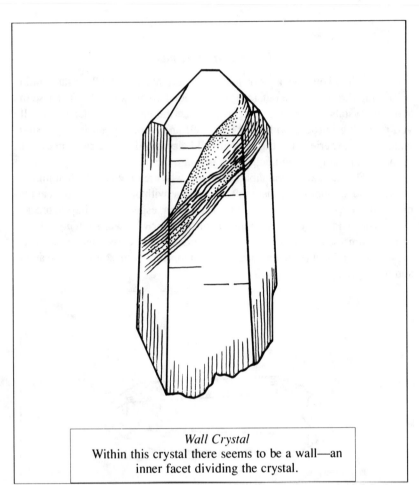

*Wall Crystal*
Within this crystal there seems to be a wall—an
inner facet dividing the crystal.

time to be alone and meditate with this crystal. It will give you insights about the situation, enabling you to see both sides of the issue, giving you some distance from it and making it easier to find a way of resolving the conflict.

If the misunderstanding is with your partner, and you're fortunate enough to be with someone who values the power of crystals, both of you can sit down facing each other and place the crystal between you. Begin by attuning to the wisdom of the crystal before speaking. Then take turns holding the crystal and speaking. Always sit in silence until the one holding the crystal feels moved to speak. Continue passing the crystal back and forth in this manner until you are both satisfied.

Swami Ty says that this crystal "divides the waters." It gives you the ability to flow along with another person and help them without getting so caught up in their problems that your own perceptions become distorted.

## Crystal Ball

This remarkable human-tooled quartz ball (as distinct from human-tooled glass balls, which are not as powerful) has the power to slide you into the past or the future. It must be used with extreme caution, particularly when looking into personal events of the future. When you see the future with today's emotions, it can be jarring and painful. If you allow events to arrive in their own time, you tend to be better prepared for them when they occur.

I use the crystal ball to help people look into events from the past that have been blocked out. I place the crystal ball at the top of a person's head while he or she is lying down, so it rests on the pillow and against the top of their head.

Then I use obsidian at the third eye (apache tears are especially appropriate when a woman has experienced sexual abuse), with two long thin delicate crystals turned toward the obsidian, charging it.

At the same time, I put two first chakra stones at the groin points for grounding; a stone at the third chakra for personal strength; another stone at the heart chakra for comfort; and a stone at the throat chakra, to make it easier to talk about the experience. I use light hypnosis to help the person to relax and go into their past. I find that using the stones in conjunction with hypnosis makes the process of recall much easier. The person has greater access to memories that have been blocked out, and the stones at the other chakras give support and reassurance.

A crystal ball is also useful for self-massage. When you have pain in your shoulders, back, buttocks, or feet, just lie on a hard surface and place the crystal ball under the painful area and roll your body over the ball, allowing it to massage the area. Visualize the crystal energy going into the painful area and irradiating it with light, draining out the pain.

A crystal ball is of great help to any group gathering, because it helps round off rough edges, making communication smoother. A crystal ball can sit atop a crystal cluster (as pictured on the cover of this book), which is perfect for certain activities, such as meditating for world peace—in which case the crystal ball symbolizes the world and the cluster symbolizes the people who are supporting her. But there are other meditations in which the energy of the people needs to reach out directly to the heaven with no intermediary, and then the crystal ball can be placed on its own separate stand.

## Channeling Crystal

This crystal has a seven-sided face in front (septagon) that is large enough to gaze into. Seven stands for intuition and wisdom. This crystal also has a perfect triangle at the opposing back side. Three is the power of speech. You can hold the seven-sided face to your third eye, with the termination toward the top of your head when you're channeling or trying to attune to the messages of the stones. It helps you to gain access to the Source of all wisdom and then it makes it easier to communicate what you've learned.

I always have my channeler with me when I do a treatment. If I reach a point where I don't know what to do, I put my channeler to my third eye and ask for guidance. The answer comes within a minute. When I ask a client to seek knowledge from their Higher Self, I hold the seven-sided face of the channeler to their third eye.

When seeking direct knowledge about gemstones or any other specific object, hold that object in one hand (usually the left, which is receptive) and with the other hand hold the channeler to your third eye. Close your eyes and go within, to seek your answer. The channeler will help you to understand and to put your understanding into words. (For more information about channeling crystals, read *Crystal Healing* by Katrina Raphaell.)

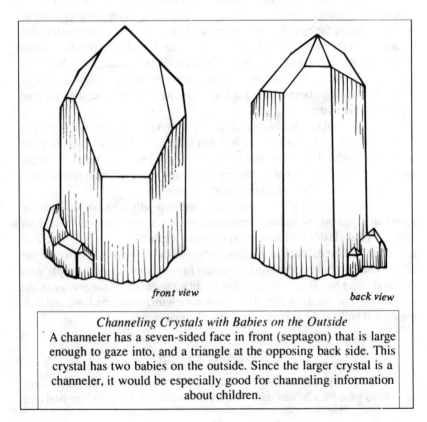

*front view*　　　　　　　　　　　　　　　　*back view*

*Channeling Crystals with Babies on the Outside*
A channeler has a seven-sided face in front (septagon) that is large enough to gaze into, and a triangle at the opposing back side. This crystal has two babies on the outside. Since the larger crystal is a channeler, it would be especially good for channeling information about children.

## *Babies on the Outside*

When there's a miniature crystal or several baby crystals on the outside of a larger crystal, these are good for people who work with children. Keep this crystal in the room or in your pocket when you're with children, and if you ever feel at a loss about how to handle a situation, touch the crystal, feel the babies and let your consciousness enter into their small bodies. You'll soon be able to move with the energy of the children, and this will help you solve the problem.

Young people are drawn to these stones, and they make nice presents for them.

# *Crystal Layouts*

The following layouts all involve clear quartz crystals as well as other kinds of stones. For more information on healing with stones, see Part IV.

The first step is to receive a treatment from a highly skilled crystal healer. Don't judge the effectiveness of crystal healing until you've received a professional treatment.

The next step is to experiment on yourself. Begin by trying the Crystal Energization described on page 35 Always lie on your back with your head to the North when doing any layout because this aligns your spine with the earth's axis and the earth's magnetic energy. Since clear quartz crystals grow naturally in veins that follow the earth's magnetic fields, and since they contain iron oxide which is a magnetic material, they're more effective when you respect their magnetic properties.

The stones may be placed over the clothing, but they're more effective when in direct contact with the skin—especially if they're small stones. The stones can be placed anywhere on or around the body, but they're usually arranged over the seven energy centers or chakras. The stones should be left in place for at least ten minutes.

After you've experienced the Crystal Energization a couple of times, place one or two stones on the appropriate chakras. Start out with one stone at a time, taking a few minutes to observe the energy of the stone and any changes that may take place in your energy. If you feel apprehensive while using the stones, remove them.

After experimenting on yourself for awhile, try to attend a workshop on crystals. This is a good way to learn more and to meet people who share your interest. Try to find someone who wants to experiment with the stones.

When you get together decide who will give and who will receive the treatment. Let the person receiving the treatment lie with his or her head to the North. If you're giving the treatment, begin by sitting in silence alongside this person, holding a toning crystal or another suitable crystal in your hand with the termination toward this person. By sitting in silence together, you allow your aura and your energy to become attuned to one another as you both attune to the energy of the crystal and to Spirit.

If you need protection, place a personal crystal or wall crystal between yourself and this person, or wear an amethyst. This is advisable when you're new to the work, or when you're feeling vulnerable, or if you sense that this person's problems are very intense or likely to trigger strong feelings in you.

Now you're ready to do a layout. Try the Chakra Balance Layout. If you feel blockages, try Charging the Chakra or Cleansing the Chakra. Try toning if you like. But don't attempt the Crystal Balancing and Toning until you're familiar with the simpler methods, and even then, only if you have good counseling skills or a strong connection with your intuition. (All these methods are described below.)

Feel free to move on to the next chakra while the stones are doing their work. Sometimes you can't clear the third chakra, for example, until you've worked on the fifth chakra. Try to stay with the person until you feel the obstructions easing away.

Don't be surprised if the person you're treating breaks out crying or becomes emotional. If you're not prepared to deal with this kind of reaction, it would be better not to attempt these layouts. The stones are very powerful.

When you do the layouts you'll be asked to feel for energy obstructions. You may think that a person would need extraordinary sensitivity to feel such a thing. But I've found in my classes that virtually everyone, often to their own surprise, can feel when their hand meets an obstruction. When this occurs, do a layout at the chakra closest to the obstruction. Then use your intuition to attune to the person and feel what they need, and proceed as described below.

## *Crystal Energization*

This simple practice has the extraordinary ability to pull out tension and negativity and then to recharge you with positive energy. It only takes ten minutes and it's better than a nap. Perhaps one day it will replace coffee.

This layout requires four clear quartz single terminated crystals. (You may substitute amethyst or smoky quartz single terminated crystals or combine them. The amethyst is best used at the head, and the smoky at the feet.) These crystals should be at least 1-1/2 inches long, but they don't have to be special or beautiful. In fact, if you do this on a bed, they're liable to fall off and get chipped, so don't use your favorite crystals for this layout.

Each crystal will have the terminations facing outward, away from the center of your body, and will be placed two to six inches from your body. Lie down on a flat surface and place the crystals in these locations:

1. above the center of the top of your head
2. between and below your feet
3. to the right of your right wrist
4. to the left of your left wrist

Lie in this position for about ten minutes. Be sure no one is in the line of fire with the terminations of the crystals. Don't worry if you fall asleep.

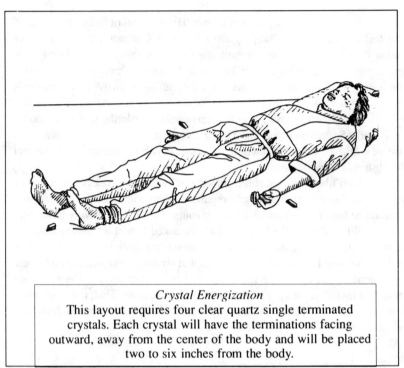

*Crystal Energization*
This layout requires four clear quartz single terminated
crystals. Each crystal will have the terminations facing
outward, away from the center of the body and will be placed
two to six inches from the body.

While doing this layout, you can simultaneously place any other stones that you feel may be beneficial for you on the appropriate parts of your body. In fact, the Crystal Energization can accompany any other treatment.

## Chakra Balance Layout

Select one stone for each chakra. You'll need two stones for the first chakra, to use at the groin points. Place the stones on the chakras. The stone at the crown chakra will lean against the top of the head.

Take a toning crystal or a single terminated clear quartz crystal and hold it in your right hand, aimed toward your client, as you sit in silence and attune your energies.

Hold your crystal a few inches above and pointing toward your client's body, beginning at the first chakra. Move your crystal very slowly through and above the central line of your client's body. As you do this, feel the energy. Ordinarily your hand will move freely, but at some point you may find that your hand simply does not want to move any further. You may feel heat or coolness or turbulent energy or a significant absence of energy.

Whatever chakra you're closest to when this occurs is the one that's likely to need work. (If you're in between two chakras, then work on both of them, using a double terminated crystal between them.) Work on the chakra by Charging the Chakra or Cleansing the Chakra, as described below.

## *Charging the Chakra*

You'll want to charge the chakra if there's an absence of energy and your hand doesn't want to move past the chakra; if it feels cool; or if you've read the description and believe that the energy there is deficient. To charge the chakra, place one stone at the center of the area where that chakra is located. Usually it will be a stone that corresponds to the chakra. (There are exceptions. For example, you may want to use the antidote—like using carnelian to close down the third eye when the energy is excessive.) Ideally, it should be a large stone.

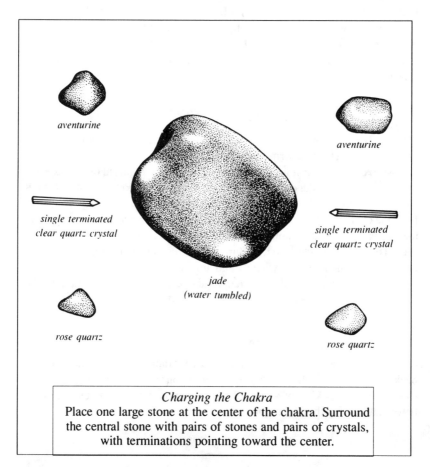

*aventurine*

*aventurine*

*single terminated clear quartz crystal*

*single terminated clear quartz crystal*

*jade*
*(water tumbled)*

*rose quartz*

*rose quartz*

*Charging the Chakra*
Place one large stone at the center of the chakra. Surround the central stone with pairs of stones and pairs of crystals, with terminations pointing toward the center.

If the situation feels quite serious, two or three stones may be used at the center, with each one on the midline of the body (so they're lined up, one on top of the other). If you're using a terminated crystal at the center of the layout (for example, a citrine crystal at the third chakra), the termination should point toward the head. Surround the central stone(s) with pairs of stones and pairs of clear quartz crystals, with terminations pointing toward the center.

Leave the stones in this arrangement for at least ten minutes, or until the end of the treatment. While they're in place, encourage your client to talk about her or his thoughts and feelings. Or you may feel the desire to tone. Or you may feel that it's time to move on and feel the energy at other chakras and return to this one later.

You may find yourself receiving images that you'll want to share with your client. Always be tentative. For example, "I'm getting an image that I'd like to share with you. If it makes sense to you, tell me. If not, just let it go." Perhaps you're getting a picture of a little girl crying in a barn. Just describe what you see, without any value judgments. "I see a little girl crying in a barn. Is that familiar to you?" You may be amazed to find that when your client was four years old, her father beat her brother with a whip, and she went out to the barn to hide.

## Cleansing the Chakra

If the energy at a particular chakra feels turbulent or hot or intense, or if you've read the description for that chakra and believe that the energy there is excessive, you'll want to cleanse that chakra to get rid of excess energy. Place a stone at the center of the area where that chakra is located. Usually it will be a stone that corresponds to that chakra, though it may be a stone from the chakra that acts as its antidote. If you're using a terminated crystal at the center (an amethyst point at the third eye for example), the termination should be pointed toward the feet. Surround the center stone with pairs of crystals (this may include smoky quartz and amethyst crystals), with terminations pointing outward. Follow the instructions above, as described for Charging the Chakra.

## Crystal Balancing

This is a powerful technique. Don't attempt it unless you have a good background in counseling and/or listening to your inner voice. If you're relatively new to this kind of work, take a workshop with a competent teacher before attempting this technique.

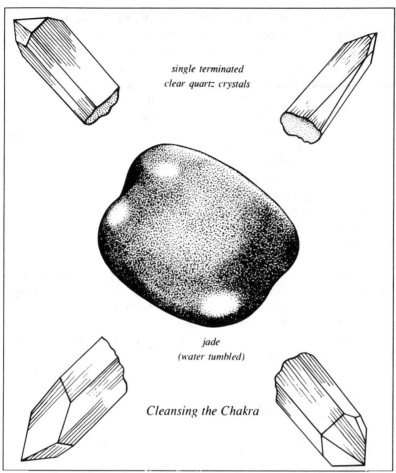

*single terminated clear quartz crystals*

*jade*
*(water tumbled)*

*Cleansing the Chakra*

Crystal Balancing requires a long toning crystal, which can be either single or double terminated. If you have a double terminated toning crystal, you'll use one end for moving counter clockwise and the other end for moving clockwise. Let the crystal guide you concerning which end to use for which movement.

Begin at the feet and move toward the head, holding the crystal at its base with the termination pointing toward each chakra. The point should be a few inches above the body. As you move from the feet to the head, relax your hand and circle the crystal in a counter-clockwise direction. When you do this, you'll be tuning in to the energy of the chakra. Your hand will get swept up in the circular movement of the chakra. You'll also be unwinding negative energy.

As you become accustomed to doing this, the movement of your hand will be flowing and unobstructed, or it may be halting, slow, irregular, or simply not moving at all. If the movement is impeded, use your various skills to work with the person (including toning, Charging the Chakra, Cleansing the Chakra, and sharing visual images as they occur to you).

The areas to work with, including the minor chakras, are:

          arch of left foot, arch of right foot
          left knee, right knee
          left hip, right hip
          first chakra
          second chakra
          third chakra
          fourth chakra
          fifth chakra
          sixth chakra
          seventh chakra

When you reach the crown chakra reverse the process, turning the crystal in a clockwise direction as you move through the same areas, going from the crown to the feet. Now you'll be bringing in positive energy. Continue working with each chakra until the spin feels normal. By the time you reach the feet (and this could take an hour or more), the person should feel totally balanced and at peace.

# PART III

---

## *The Seven Chakras*

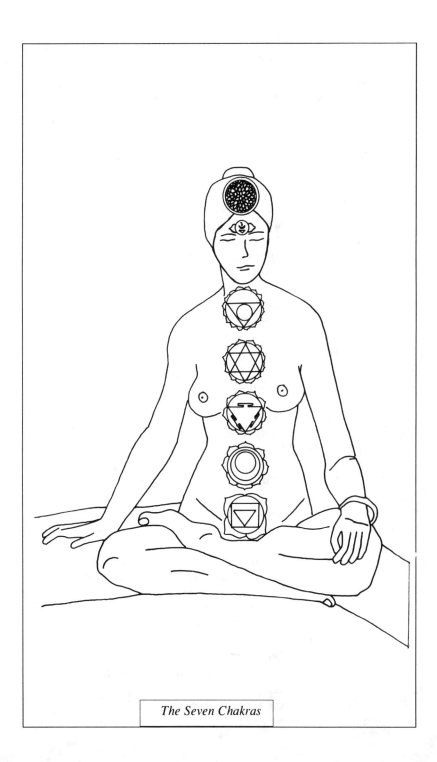

*The Seven Chakras*

# Table of Chakras and Stones

Within this book, I have categorized the crystals and other stones under the chakras where I use them most frequently. However, some stones are commonly used for two or more chakras. The color of the stone will often—but not always—correspond to the color associated with that chakra. All of the stones can be used at any part of the body. The following chart shows the chakras at which I most frequently use the stones mentioned in this book.

*FIRST CHAKRA —Red*
  red garnet
  black obsidian
  smoky quartz
*SECOND CHAKRA —Orange*
  tiger's eye
  carnelian
*THIRD CHAKRA —Yellow*
  citrine
  turquoise
  malachite
*FOURTH CHAKRA —Green*
  green jade
  green aventurine
  rose quartz
  watermelon tourmaline
  malachite
*FIFTH CHAKRA —Blue*
  sodalite
  azurite
  lapis
  clear quartz crystal
*SIXTH CHAKRA —Indigo*
  lapis
  sodalite
  purple, blue, white or gold fluorite
  sugilite (luvulite)
  amethyst
  clear quartz crystal
*SEVENTH CHAKRA —Violet*
  lapis
  purple, blue, white or gold fluorite
  amethyst
  clear quartz crystal

The next section on the chakras is organized under key words, which are explained below. Before reading the section on the chakras, read through the following definitions. Just skim over the parts that don't make sense; as you read the chakra section it will begin to fit into place, and you can return to the key words and read them again for greater clarity.

## *Chakra*

Chakra (also spelled cakra) means wheel or vortex. A chakra is an invisible (to the normal human eye) center of spinning energy. Through the chakras, we're able to receive and transmit social, sexual, and spiritual energy. In the system I use, there are seven chakras. Some schools say there are six, and some say five. Yet there is a surprising amount of agreement about where they are, and what their functions are.

People who have inner vision can actually see or feel the chakras. You may be able to do this yourself: lie on your back and pass your hand over your front midline, from the pubic area to the top of your head, a few inches above your body. You may feel the chakras as intense concentrations of energy. And you may see the colors of the chakras with your third eye, even if you aren't looking directly at them (it may be easier to do this with your eyes closed). You can also try to see the colors of a friend's chakra.

The first three chakras are below the chest: these are called the lower chakras. The heart chakra at the chest and the top three chakras are called the higher chakras.

I believe that when our spirits enter our bodies, usually when the body is still in the womb, all our chakras are open. Newborn babies who are truly wanted and who experience a natural birth tend to be unarmored, energetic, and completely in tune with All That Is. But even in the womb, many of us experience a closing off of these energy centers. Rejection can be experienced even before birth.

The chakras tend to close down from the top downward. In my work with hypnotherapy, I have seen that most of my clients closed down the top three chakras by the time they were three years old, as a reaction to the disbelief of their parents and society (disbelief in nature spirits, in spirit friends, and in past lives). During the teen-age years, the heart chakra often closed down (or became imbalanced) because of pain and rejection from parents, peers, and lovers. The third chakra often closed down (or became imbalanced) when parents and society forced teens into molds that didn't fit. By the time they entered adulthood, many of them had closed down all but the first two chakras. The closure of a chakra doesn't ordinarily occur in response to a single event; rather it's the repetition of similar events without relief that eventually leads to closing off the chakra.

After high school, there is often less pressure to conform. Some of them began to reverse the process and started opening their chakras. Usually the third chakra opened before the fourth, and all the chakras opened in succession going upward. But that isn't always true. For example, I've worked with people who were spiritually developed (because of work they did in past lives) who came from difficult family situations and who had little sense of self-worth. These people didn't need to work on their higher chakras to become whole; they needed to work on their lower chakras.

In reality, the concept of open or closed chakras is an oversimplification, since there are various degrees of openness that can be experienced at different chakras. According to Swami Tayumanavar, there are seven stages of openness for each chakra, and all the chakras are at least slightly open (the first one-seventh) in every human being.

The assignment of different illnesses, ailments and emotions to particular chakras is also somewhat artificial. In fact, there is (and should be) a great deal of flow between the chakras; it's only our minds that need to put things into categories.

Some authorities believe that as people raise their consciousness, the higher chakras open and the lower chakras close. I prefer to envision higher consciousness as being an opening of all the chakras.

Dr. Laing says, "In a highly evolved person, the chakras are like progressively larger fountains, with the yellow of personal power tumbling over the orange of sexuality, which is brimming over the small but brilliant red of a firm foundation."

## Names

The concept of the chakras has been in existence longer than recorded history. In this category I give the most common names for the chakras, beginning with the ancient Sanskrit names (and their translations).

## Symbol

According to Hindu tradition, each chakra has a symbol. There are many different versions of these symbols, which often include great detail. I've given simple versions of the traditional symbols. Each chakra is shown within a circle surrounded by lotus petals. The circle represents the spinning wheel of energy within the chakra, and the lotus petals represent the gradual awakening of the whole self, finally culminating in the fully opened lotus at the seventh chakra.

My interpretations are a combination of what I've read and my own intuition.

## Location

This tells exactly where the chakra is anatomically located. There are differences of opinion on the location of the chakras, but considering how ancient this knowledge is and how many cultures it spans, there's a remarkable degree of agreement. I've given the locations that seem right to me.

## Color

Each chakra has a particular color. Various systems assign different colors to the chakras. I've used the rainbow system beginning with red at the first chakra and ending with violet at the crown chakra.

## Antidotes

An antidote counteracts the effect of a substance, as hot antidotes cold and cold antidotes hot. The colors and characteristics of the three lower chakras can be antidoted by those of the three upper chakras, and vice versa. The center (heart) chakra is balanced and needs no antidote. These are the antidotes for the colors of the chakras:

Red antidotes blue and blue antidotes red.

Orange antidotes indigo and indigo antidotes orange.

Yellow antidotes violet and violet antidotes yellow.

This concept is essential in color healing, as can be seen in this statement from Dr. Laing: "If a baby's skin is too red, then it is overly excited. This condition should be watched closely, because it can become habitual and lead to red conditions such as heart troubles and high blood pressure in later life. If the baby's mother learns to handle it in early life, these patterns can be changed.

"Help the baby to relax. To do this, help the mother to relax. Impress upon her that her relaxation is good for the baby. Give her plenty of blue light. Put her under a blue lamp. Have her wear blue clothes. Listen to soothing music. Bring in blue flowers. Create a soothing environment."

## Tone and Note

Each chakra vibrates at a different frequency or vibration and on a different note. When you chant the tone on the given note, this should vibrate the chakra, awakening and opening it. If you find that you can achieve the same effect by using a different tone and a different note, feel free to use it.

## Element

Each chakra corresponds with one of the elements such as earth, air, fire and water.

## Sense

Each chakra corresponds to a different sense such as smell, taste and touch.

## Statements

The succinct phrases in this category were received during meditation when I asked my own chakras to speak and describe themselves to me. I've found that on different days (and for different people) they respond differently. These "statements" can be used as loose (and sometimes amusing) guidelines. Try it yourself.

## Explanation

In this category I describe the essential energy of the chakra, often quoting from Dr. Laing and *The Book of Guidance*.

## Tarot Archetype

An archetype is a basic personality type present in the racial subconscious of each individual. The Tarot Trumps can be seen as classic archetypes. Dr. Laing assigned one or two Trumps to each chakra. Those who are familiar with the Tarot will find this a rich way of grasping the energy of these chakras. When all our chakras are open, we have full access to each of these archetypes, as personified in the seventh chakra Trump of The Fool.

## Balanced, Excessive and Deficient Energy

When the energy is strong, open, and balanced, it flows through each chakra. When your childhood and adolescence have been healthy and nurturing, you may be balanced and open in every chakra.

But when there is unreleased emotion such as fear or anger accumulated from years of past experience, and when there's been a lack of nourish-

48

ment and encouragement during the developmental period, the energy flows less freely to these centers. On the other hand, when a child is confronted with aggressive or disapproving behavior, he or she may respond by becoming aggressive or by assuming a superior attitude, resulting in excessive energy. People with either of these symptoms are imbalanced in their chakras. This is not unusual. Rather, the balanced individuals are unusual in our society.

Many of the examples of personality types may sound like stereotypes, but they're all descriptions of actual people. These portraits are given because they're easier to visualize and remember than a list of characteristics. The sexes and the professions can be reversed. Not all of the characteristics need apply.

You may get a mixture of excessive and deficient characteristics in one person, or an individual may swing back and forth between excessive and deficient, sometimes passing through a temporary balance. But when the energy in a chakra is clearly excessive, it can be treated with the antidote, or the color of a higher chakra. If it's deficient, it should be treated with the color of that chakra.

For example, sexual energy comes mostly from the second chakra which is orange, so someone with excessive sexual energy may benefit from the antidote, which is indigo. This color will calm the sexual energy, making the person feel less nervous. An alternate treatment is to use yellow which strengthens the third chakra, putting the person more in touch with his or her personal gift which in turn enhances feelings of self-worth, making this person less desperate for a sexual partner.

The personality will usually reflect either the energy of the highest open chakra or the chakra with the most energy and focus. For example, I see Beethoven as a fifth chakra personality and I imagine that this may have been his highest open chakra. On the other hand, I see Mozart as a balanced second chakra personality, because while his third, fourth and fifth chakras were certainly open, he seems to have enjoyed focusing much of his energy through his second chakra. As Laing says, "When an evolved and balanced person focuses energies through a lower chakra, the color of that chakra will glimmer in their aura, in a particularly crystalline hue."

Under the balanced personalities of each chakra, I've mentioned various religions. I have not tried to designate religions for those who are out of balance, nor have I attempted to mention every religion.

These categories are to be taken very loosely. The same religion may be practiced by people who are focused at different chakras. For example, I placed Judaism at the third chakra, because of the Jewish devotion to The Law and The Word and because of the great love that Jews have for good food. However, there is a high form of Hasidic Judaism that is full of ecstatic song and dance, which is a fourth or seventh chakra experience, depending on who practices it or how intense the ecstasy becomes.

Similarly, I put American Indian religions at the first chakra, because of their deep connection with the earth, but there are shamans (medicine people) who are fully self realized, who express their spirituality through the sixth or seventh chakras.

When sexuality is described for a person who is balanced, this is the expression of someone who may also be open at higher chakras but whose main focus is through that chakra. When I describe the sexuality of a person who is out of balance, I am referring to the person who is open at that chakra but not necessarily at the higher chakras.

## Contraindications

People who have the listed symptoms should not use the color of that chakra.

## Glands and Organs Influenced by the Chakra

Each chakra will have an influence over the endocrine glands and internal organs that are located in the part of the body where that chakra is located. Sometimes the influence will cover a broader sphere, as happens with the first chakra, which is located at the tail bone and which rules not only the bladder, vagina, and male reproductive organs but also the blood and the spine. The endocrine glands for the first chakra are at the male testes.

## Illnesses and Ailments

The illnesses and ailments that are given will respond well to treatment with the color of that chakra, and they may also respond to the gemstones and the tones of that chakra. Instructions on how to use color, gemstones and toning can be found in the instruction section at the back of the book.

## Stones

These are various crystals and other stones that have been arranged according to the chakras where they're most commonly used (see the Table on page 44).

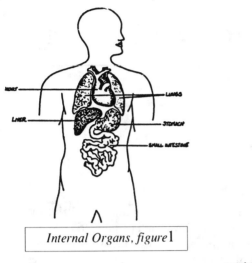

*Internal Organs, figure* 1

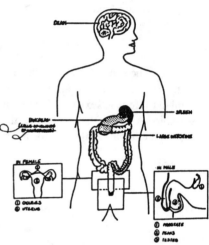

*Internal Organs, figure 2*

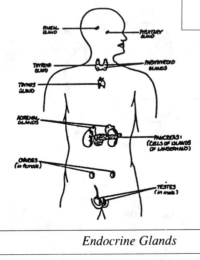

*Endocrine Glands*

# First Chakra

## Names

Muladhara (Support)
Kundalini Center
Root Chakra
Base Chakra

## Symbol

The symbol for the first chakra is a square (yantra), symbolizing the earth, the foundation. Within the square is a downward pointing triangle, the symbol for female sexuality. Within the triangle is a linga, the symbol for male sexuality. A snake, the symbol for the kundalini, coils three-and-a-half times around the linga. On the outside are four lotus petals.

## Location

at the tailbone

## Color

red
*Antidote*, blue

## Tone

e (as in red)
*Note*, c

## Element

earth

## Sense

smell

## Statement

"I want stuff."

## Explanation

The first chakra concerns your connection with the earth, your birthplace, your culture, your foundations. The first chakra is influenced by your earliest relationships. If there was one person who gave you unconditional love, you're likely to have a strong first chakra, and your survival mechanism will be good. If you didn't receive unconditional love, your first chakra will probably be weak.

This is the center of physical energy and vitality. It's grounded in material reality, so this is the center of manifestation. When you're trying to make things happen in the material world, in business or material possessions, the energy to succeed will come from the first chakra.

According to *The Book of Guidance* (slightly rephrased), "The dazzling red will intensify whatever you are feeling. It will warm and speed up the molecules. It is the color of passion. It is used sparingly in the flowers, and only for emphasis in the sunsets. It is used to arouse attention and interest. There is balance when red is used sparingly. Do not cut yourself off from passion .... It has its place. It is a source of power and self-confidence, which you should always have access to. It is an intensity of energy and anger which is frightening or disturbing to many.

"But if you are to be whole, then you will need access to this part of your nature. You may at times need to act forcefully, as a warrior, to defend that which you love. You may need to summon great strength, to move through a difficult situation.

"But red is frightening to many people, because they have seen the damage that can be done when it gets out of hand.

"The red of fire has brought both warmth and misery. The red of anger enables us to feel both intensity and pain. The red of confidence can erupt into egotism and exhibitionism. The red of passion can turn to greed.

"Each feeling contains atomic particles, and the feelings which are denied contain particles which spin at a greater force than normal because their natural movement has been suppressed. This greater intensity of spin creates the color, red. When there is a large accumulation of these particles, the energy can no longer be contained, which results in an explosive force which you perceive as violence. This may express itself as a tantrum, as abrasive behavior, belligerence, insult, physical abuse, rape, or even murder. 'Seeing red' is an actual phenomenon.

"This expression of violence often occurs when the use of alcohol or drugs has removed the usual social inhibitions that prevent their expression. An alternate route is indirect expression through illness. Then the violence is expressed through red as inflammation. Nearly every illness involves some aspect of inflammation."

## Tarot Archetype

### The Hermit

This card shows a figure in a red robe, head turned away, walking through a field grown high with wheat, moving toward the blue sky where an egg is surrounded by a snake. Rays of light shine down upon him, and he carries a brilliant lantern. His hand holds the lantern in the center of the card. At the bottom left is a spermatozoon and at the bottom right is Cerberus, the three-headed Hound of Hell.

The wheat symbolizes his connection with nature, fertility, and abundance. He's the European version of the shaman. He goes into the wilderness and lives alone, turning away from social interaction. Yet he extends a helping hand to all who need him.

The hermit wears a red robe. Red is the color of the first chakra. In India, the Tantric adept wears red, symbolizing that person's ability to transmute sexual energy, using it to arouse the kundalini, which is symbolized by

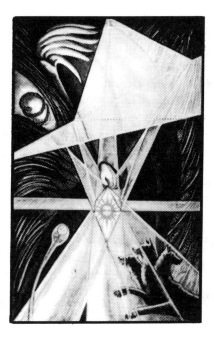

the spermatozoon, the apparently tame Cerberus, the egg and the snake—
which is akin to the Hindu lingam, the symbol for the kundalini.

The Hebrew letter for this card is Yod which means the hand of God.
The hand at the center of the card holds the lamp; it lights the way. The hermit
pursues enlightenment and his visions enrich the community.

### Balanced Energy in First Chakra

*Characteristics*
> centered
> grounded
> master of yourself
> healthy
> fully alive
> unlimited physical energy
> can manifest abundance
> spiritual expression could be
>> Celtic
>> an American Indian religion
>> an African tribesperson's religion
>> Hatha Yoga

sexual energy:
> affectionate
> able to trust and be vulnerable
> sensuality is felt throughout your body

*Example*

This native Indian medicine woman and midwife expresses her spirituality through seasonal rituals which involve specific places in nature, use of herbs, dancing, and chanting. Her eyes sparkle and though she is in her seventies she walks and laughs like a young woman. She has plenty of energy and always knows what to do.

## Excessive Energy in First Chakra

*Characteristics*
> egotistic
> domineering
> greedy
> addicted to wealth
> sexual energy:
>> indiscriminate
>> focus is entirely genital
>> nervous sexual energy
>> may be sadistic

*Example*

This wealthy perfectionist is the owner of a California restaurant chain. He rules his employees like a demanding general. He is nervous and chronically constipated. He owns three cars, which give him little satisfaction. He sleeps with many women, but it's an empty experience.

## Deficient Energy in First Chakra

*Characteristics*
> lack confidence
> can't get your feet on the ground
> weak
> can't achieve goals
> self-destructive, suicidal
> sexual energy:
>> feel unlovable
>> fear being abandoned
>> have little interest in sex
>> masochistic

56

This unskilled, insecure woman lives in a chaotic house and spends most of her time watching television. Her parents were alcoholic. She's under-weight and often forgets to eat. She's chronically depressed, has no energy and little interest in men. Life holds no pleasure for her.

## *Contraindications*

Avoid red for all nervous and red conditions.
agitated
hyperactive
fever
ulcers
high blood pressure
red face
swellings
inflammations

CAUTION: If you use red light on your head, limit the treatment to three minutes and apply a cool wet cloth or a blue cloth to your head during the treatment or for at least two minutes afterwards. Red is the most potent color, the easiest to overdose with. If you feel nervous, angry, hot, or uneasy while sitting under this light, discontinue it. Use blue light as an antidote.

## *Glands and Organs Influenced by the First Chakra*

blood
spine
nervous system
bladder
male reproductive organs
testes
vagina

NOTE: A man's sexual organs are located primarily in his first chak-ra, so male sexual energy is usually experienced primarily as physical. A woman's sexual organs are located primarily in her second chakra, so female sexual energy is usually experienced primarily as emotional. Both chakras are associated with sexual energy.

## Illnesses and Ailments to be Treated with Red

Since red is the antidote for blue, it will be used to treat blue conditions. Since it's stimulating, it will be used to treat slow and weak conditions. Since it's in the first chakra area, it will be used to treat organs which are located in the lower region of the body. Since it is red, it can be used to cleanse and build up the blood.

depressed, fearful
debilitated, lack of energy
spaced out, ungrounded
low blood pressure
bladder infections
sluggish digestion
inactive, flaky skin
shock
anemia
poor circulation
impotence, frigidity
infertility
no menstrual period
after childbirth, if weak
(or if there's been much blood loss)
menopause, if weak
(alternate with longer doses of blue if there are hot flashes)

## Stones

### Red Garnet

This stone has an arousing, invigorating energy. It influences the kundalini energy that rises up the spine. Therefore it relates to the base chakra and to the sixth chakra.

Garnets are commonly found as small blood-colored stones. Small stones are easily misplaced and not terribly powerful, but you can take an ordinary single terminated crystal and mount a small garnet cabochon on the main face of the crystal. Then the energy of the garnet combines with the sending power of the crystal, and the effect is excellent. This can be done easily with the strong glue jewelers use, along with a separate hardener that must be mixed with the glue just before using.

When placed on the third eye (while lying on your back), the garnet facilitates past life recall. A plain garnet or a garnet ring or pendant can be used, or a garnet mounted on a crystal.

To improve fertility, a woman can lie on her back and place the garnet over her womb area. This is also a good placement for menstrual cramps, irregular periods, and during menopause. A man can place garnets at his groin points (where the thighs meet the torso) to improve his fertility. These treatments can be repeated daily for at least ten minutes for a week or two.

For low back pains and premenstrual cramps, lie on your stomach and place the red garnet at your lower back. This is also a good placement if you want to cleanse the blood or to improve circulation. It's most effective if you use a large garnet or several small ones.

When wearing the garnet, it is best worn below the waist. When above the waist, it can overstimulate the solar plexus or the pituitary in sensitive individuals, causing nervousness, headaches or dizziness.

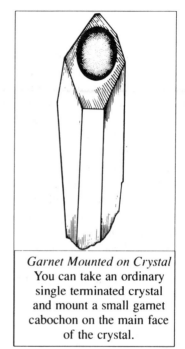

*Garnet Mounted on Crystal*
You can take an ordinary single terminated crystal and mount a small garnet cabochon on the main face of the crystal.

### Black Obsidian

Obsidian comes from lava which has cooled quickly. Basalt obsidian is glassy and black, yet when you hold it to the light, you can see through all but the densest obsidian. Obsidian is good for those who feel cut off from the Source of Light. By gazing into the obsidian and then holding it to the light, you will be reminded that even when you feel dark and cut off, the inner light can always shine through.

Obsidian is a wonderful stone for grounding. Dark stones connect with the earth energy, so they keep you connected with your body. People who have intense emotional or spiritual experiences often find it difficult to return to the normal world. It's hard for them to integrate what they've experienced into their day-to-day lives. To assist these people. I place obsidian at the groin points to help them keep their feet on the ground, so they won't feel too spaced out. They'll be better able to integrate what they've learned, and they'll be able to drive home safely.

This stone cleanses toxins from the liver, so it's good for people who are exposed to environmental pollutants. This is one way of dealing with anger because anger is held in the liver. But if you've been repressing anger, it's best to begin by finding a way to release your anger physically—without hurting

...nyone. You might try running or chopping wood or hitting pillows while allowing yourself to think about the person you're angry at.

To cleanse the liver, place a large piece (ideally, about the size of your fist, though a smaller piece may be used) over your liver (which lies beneath the lower part of your right rib cage). Allow ten to thirty minutes for a treatment. Afterwards, you may find yourself feeling remarkably light and happy.

This is a potent remedy. People who've used it have found that it can produce diarrhea, bad breath, phlegm from the lungs, and nasal discharge. When people have fallen asleep and left it on overnight, they reported an uncomfortable amount of discharge. Be sure to bury the obsidian for at least twenty-four hours after each treatment.

The same method may be used over the spleen, which is where worry and grief are held. Your spleen lies beneath your left rib cage. After treating the spleen, you may find yourself crying and discharging old emotions that you've held onto for a long time.

Apache tears are smooth, irregularly rounded chunks of obsidian. According to legend, all the Apache warriors were wiped out in a battle on a particular mountain. When the women found them, the foot of the mountain was covered with these chunks of black obsidian.

I call these Apache tears womb stones. The obsidian represents the darkness of the womb—it helps women to feel good about their reproductive organs. A woman can place the obsidian over her womb when she's lying down. She can imagine white moonlight shining from the dark sky into the obsidian, and radiating through her womb, charging it with the power of darkness. This is important, because there's too much association between darkness and negativity.

I don't recommend wearing obsidian as a pendant over the heart because it prevents the easy flow of energy in and out of the heart. However, there may be times when you want to seal off your heart and the obsidian is better than building walls, since it's easier to remove.

Be careful about wearing obsidian, because it can draw other people's darkness to you. If you feel it has done this, bury the stone in sand or dirt for a few days before wearing it again.

An obsidian ring can be worn by a person of power, and it can be a pleasant source of mystery and intrigue. In India, the women wear obsidian toe rings. This is a good way to stay grounded. It pulls negative energy down to the feet and then sends it into the earth.

### Smoky Quartz

This stone has a positive force, a strong electrical charge, which gives it the ability to disperse dark energies. Though it appears to be dark, it is translucent when held to the light. Similarly, our bodies appear to be dense, yet we can meditate and bathe in the light of Spirit. Smoky quartz helps us to do this.

It brings the white energy of the crown down to the base chakra, helping us to accept and feel good about every aspect of ourselves.

This brown quartz crystal is powerful when used at any part of the body. The stones that appear very dark are the most powerful. Smoky quartz derives its dark color from exposure to natural radioactivity. Imitation smoky quartz is made by artificially radiating clear quartz. The artificially radiated stones are very dark, and not translucent. I wouldn't use them for healing.

Place the smoky quartz wherever you feel physical, emotional, or psychic blocks. Surround it with clear quartz crystals, pointing outward to disperse negativity.

Since pain is often caused by negative emotions such as resentment and anger, you can disperse pain if you place smoky quartz over the painful area and allow yourself to get in touch with the source of the pain.

Use it in a room where there are actual or potential negative energies, such as jealousy, resentment, or deliberate confusion. It will thicken those energies so that they become heavy and merge with the earth. Then they don't have the power to rise and cause trouble. Use it in a room where people tend to be belligerent or unreasonable. To purify the energies in a room before, during, or after the room has been used, place one piece of smoky quartz at each corner of the room, with the terminations pointing outward, to disperse negative energies.

When treating an individual, if a person is holding onto negativity that needs to be released, lean a smoky quartz crystal against each heel, with the terminations pointing downward. This helps to pull the negativity down through their legs and feet, and then directs that energy toward the earth, which disperses it. On the other hand, if a person is too spaced out and needs more grounding, place the smoky quartz crystals against each heel, with the terminations pointing toward the toes. This pulls energy up from the earth and directs it into the body.

I use this stone for people who are struggling with fears, nightmares, strange visions, or anything they regard as evil. Fear usually migrates to a particular part of the body which reflects that which is feared. For example, I used smoky quartz for a nun who developed a pain in her right knee. She was feeling angry and rebellious toward the head priest. Her right knee was the one she bowed down upon in church.

I put the smoky quartz over the painful part of the body with the termination pointing toward the head, and I encouraged the person to talk. Soon the skeleton is out of the closet, old fears (often related to childhood incidents) lose their potency, and the fear and pain are dispersed.

Smoky quartz is associated with the first chakra because of its powerful connection with the earth. On the other hand, clear quartz crystals are associated with the crown chakra because they embody the White Light. If I hold

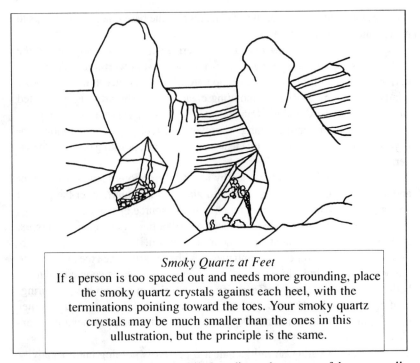

*Smoky Quartz at Feet*
If a person is too spaced out and needs more grounding, place the smoky quartz crystals against each heel, with the terminations pointing toward the toes. Your smoky quartz crystals may be much smaller than the ones in this ullustration, but the principle is the same.

a clear quartz crystal in my hand while I meditate, the energy of the stone pulls me up and lightens me. It carries me toward the light. When I meditate with smoky quartz my third eye feels activated, my consciousness expands, and part of my energy becomes heavy and sinks into the ground where it connects with the earth energy.

Smoky quartz is ideal for practical people: scientists, geologists, and teachers who must keep their feet on the ground but still enjoy taking excursions into the outer realms.

This is a wonderful stone to use after channeling, inner healing, past-life explorations, or astral travel. Hold it in your hand while you sit in quiet meditation, and it will bring you in for a smooth landing on planet earth.

As jewelry, smoky quartz is not appropriate for casual wear, though it can be worn regularly by those who are aware of its energy. It can be worn effectively for ceremonial purposes, particularly for ceremonies which involve the earth. When you wear smoky quartz, it pulls your energies down, making you feel heavy. But there are some people (usually very spiritual people) who require this sort of anchor. They may be seen smoking cigarettes or doing something that seems strangely out of character. For these people, just wearing smoky quartz or keeping a hunk of it in their pocket may alleviate the need for less desirable substances.

# Second Chakra

## Names

Svadisthana (Abode of the Vital Force)
Sacral Center
Splenic Chakra

## Symbol

The crescent moon symbolizes receptivity and the womb. It is the symbol of femininity. On the outside are six lotus petals.

## Location

1-2 inches below navel or
branching to left side at spleen

Most people have a concentration of orange energy an inch or two below the navel. But for some people (particularly those who have chosen to be celibate) this chakra will branch off to the left side of the body and locate under the left rib cage at the spleen, which is why this is sometimes called the splenic chakra. Then it will have a blue-green color.

## *Color*

orange (below navel)
blue-green (at spleen)
> *Antidote*, indigo

## *Tone*

o (as in home)
*Note*, d

## *Element*

water

## *Sense*

taste

## *Statement*

"I desire" (This could relate to money or sex or God, or anything else.)

## *Explanation*

The second chakra is about friendliness, creativity, sexuality, and emotions and intuition. The second chakra governs people's sense of self-worth, their confidence in their own creativity, and their ability to relate to others in an open and friendly way. It's influenced by how emotions were expressed or repressed in your family during your childhood.

Orange is a sociable color since it combines the physical red with the intellectual yellow, so it's good to use in living rooms and family rooms, classrooms, and social areas in hospitals. But use a light orange because the red in reddish orange can be overstimulating and create nervousness.

It's rumored that the reason why one popular fast-food chain has bright orange and pink seats is because the pink attracts customers, and the orange is friendly but it keeps the customers energized so they don't want to relax and stay too long.

The second chakra is the center of the emotions and it's in the area of the large intestines. Consequently, when you feel emotionally imbalanced, you're likely to experience diarrhea or constipation.

This is the center of gut-level intuition. Since a woman's womb is at the second chakra, it may explain why this is often called women's intuition. It's a basic visceral feeling. "I just knew it was going to rain," and "I had a feeling you were going to call," are statements that typify the second chakra intuition. (There's another kind of intuition that's found at the sixth chakra.)

The second chakra is the sexual center particularly for women, because the uterus, fallopian tubes, and ovaries are located here. This may be one reason why women tend to be more emotional about sexual relations. When the second chakra has a healthy spin, it usually indicates that this person has a healthy sex life or at least a healthy attitude toward sex. *The Book of Guidance* says, "Fill your sexual organs with radiant acceptance. Feel your sexual desires finding union with your spiritual desires.

"Herein lies the Mystery of Mysteries. Desire itself is the Divine Motivator. Sexual energy is required to fire all other energy....

"The orange energy gives you the ability to reach out, to radiate, to extend yourself. It gives you the forcefulness to reach *up*—to your heart, and to your soul.

"Regard your sexual center as a precious fountainhead of vital energy. Explore that energy, learn to channel it, and eventually you will learn to use it as a part of your Total Self, to achieve whatever goal you seek...."

## *Tarot Archetype*

Two cards describe the second chakra.

### *The Lovers*

Here we see the attraction of opposites. When your spiritual and sexual development are at the second chakra level, you attempt to find fulfillment through union with your opposite. This inevitably leads to conflict because your opposite represents the part of yourself that you have difficulty accepting.

Here we see the dark male holding the sword (which represents the intellect) while the dark child holds the club (which represents physical touch and sensuality). There is also a dark lingam-egg representing rebirth and transformation. Meanwhile, the light female holds the cup (emotional communication and attachment) and the light child holds the flowers (the spiritual bond).

The figures are being blessed by a looming figure whose face is obscured and whose arms appear to be tied, which gives a sense of inevitability

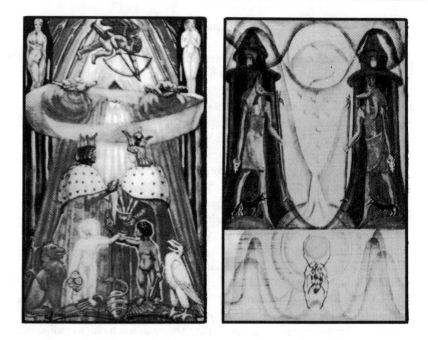

about this union of opposites. Above this figure is a blindfolded cupid representing blind fate, or karma, the true intentions of which are not visible to the couple. Above them all are swords like prison bars representing difficulties and responsibilities, conflicts and commitments.

The Hebrew letter for this card is Zain, which means sword, division, separation.

### The Moon

This card represents subconscious urges and the reptilian, primitive, instinctive consciousness. It shows tides being moved by the moon, which suggests emotional and sexual responses upon which the intellect has no control.

The card abounds in sexual imagery. Two phallic towers stand at either side of a vaginal path. Below this is a womb-like circle. Embracing the circle is a scarab which represents regeneration and healing. This could be the Life Path as seen from the womb.

Two men with heads of jackals guard the path. The jackals represent an opportunity to clean up old carrion, karma from the past. Each sentry holds a key shaped like the astrological symbol for Mercury. Since Mercury rules the intellect, this seems to say, "The price of entering here is your mind."

The Hebrew letter is Qoph, which means the back of the head where subconscious thoughts lie buried.

## Balanced Energy in Second Chakra

*Characteristics*

> friendly, optimistic
> concerned for others
> sense of belonging
> creative, imaginative
> intuitive
> clairsentient: can become one with another person and psyche them
>> out in order to better understand them
> attuned to your own feelings
> gutsy sense of humor
> spiritual expression could be
>> Pentecostal
>> Rajneesh style yoga
> sexual energy:
>> highest goal is to have a wonderful orgasm
>> may desire children

*Example*

Mozart (as portrayed in the movie, *Amadeus*) is a delightful example of a man who has a well-developed second chakra. He is friendly, jovial, self-confident, courageous and outrageous. He actively pursues his own creativity. He writes raucous, unconventional, "immoral" operas and falls in love with a beautiful, sexy young woman whom he marries despite the fact that she is beneath his class.

## Excessive Energy in Second Chakra

*Characteristics*

> emotionally explosive
> aggressive
> overly ambitious
> manipulative
> caught up in illusion
> overindulgent
> self-serving
> clairsentient (see above), but can't distinguish between your own
>> feelings and the feelings of other people
> sexual energy:

67

        obsessed with thoughts of sex
        see people as sex objects
        require frequent sexual gratification

*Example*

        This woman works as a fashion model and sells cosmetics on the side. She's obsessed with her appearance and spends most of her money on clothes, jewelry, and perfumes. She values herself according to how much attention she receives from men. She's constantly looking at men's bodies and comparing them to her ideal of the perfect male. She uses men to get what she wants and when she can't get what she wants, she blows up.

## Deficient Energy in Second Chakra

*Characteristics*

        extremely shy, timid
        immobilized by fear
        overly sensitive
        self-negating
        resentful
        bury your emotions
        burdened by guilt
        distrustful
        sexual energy:
                clinging
                guilty about having sex
                difficulty conceiving
                abused
                frigid or impotent

*Example*

        This fellow is shy and retiring, gentle and thoughtful. Secretly he thinks that sex is crude and often suffers from impotence.

## Contraindications

        excessive energy
        excessive sexual energy

## Glands and Organs Influenced by the Second Chakra

        skin
        mammary glands (milk is produced through ovarian hormones)
        female reproductive organs
        kidneys

68

## Illnesses and Ailments to be Treated with Orange

kidney weakness
constipation
muscle cramps and spasms
insufficient lactation
lack of energy
allergies (hypersensitive to environment)
repression and inhibition

## Stones

### Tiger's Eye

This stone is an opener. It's often the first stone that attracts your attention. Children are often drawn to tiger's eye. It's tactile—it speaks to the sense of touch—and it gives comfort through its cool smoothness which is in strange contrast to its velvety appearance.

You don't need to be intellectual or spiritual to enjoy the qualities of tiger's eye. It connects you to the rich browns of the earth, and it blends that energy with the gold of the Divine Light. Bring this stone to your third eye and it will help you to see the best in everyone and to feel happy about walking on the path of life.

This is a stone of courage. It gives strength and endurance and the willingness to go forward in spite of obstacles. By stroking its smooth surface you'll soothe away your worries and apprehensions.

This is a sensuous stone which is often favored as a gift between lovers. Since our emotions are so connected to our sexuality, thoughts about sex and love can cause anxiety and nervous tension. This in turn causes the energy at the second chakra to spin irregularly or in an agitated pattern. To calm your mind and restore your energy to its normal spin, hold the tiger's eye and gaze at the striped pattern, and then place this stone at your second chakra.

You can wear tiger's eye as a ring or necklace or carry it in your pocket. If you are in a relationship, it will help you to tune into your partner in a telepathic way.

### Carnelian

Carnelian is a red-orange agate which generates warmth and relaxation. It has a strong masculine energy and is good for the sexual organs and for sexual energy. It's the ginseng of the gemstones. (Ginseng is a herb valued by the Chinese for toning up the male sexual organs and enhancing virility.) It can be used over the sexual organs or at the groin points when there is physical pain or when you feel hurt by a lover.

I use it when a person is holding tension in a particular part of their body. It works like a tiny heating pad, bringing warmth to the area and allowing the tension to ease away. It works well for tension in the shoulders and between the shoulder blades.

Carnelian can be placed over the second chakra for a sluggish digestion.

Since orange and indigo are antidotes for each other, carnelian can be used when the sixth chakra (indigo) has excessive energy. For example, if you're experiencing intense unsolicited past life recall and you can't take the time to relax into it, you can use carnelian at your third eye to close down the sixth chakra energy. You can combine it with two delicate quartz crystals pointing away from the carnelian to discharge the energy. This will enable you to calm down and get grounded.

When all the energy is in your higher chakras and you feel out of balance or, when there is an untimely or premature rising of the kundalini, two carnelian stones may be placed at the groin points. This will be effective in balancing out the energy.

Children are drawn to this stone because it gives strength, humor and optimism. Just having a stone in their pocket will counter any tendency toward depression, negativity, or belligerence. (It won't necessarily eliminate these behaviors, but it will diminish them.)

This is the stone of worldly success. It grounds you in the present and gives protection against negative energy. It gives the wearer courage to speak out. Business people can wear this stone or carry it in their pockets, especially below their waists.

Carnelian is fiery, intense and assertive. It will enhance your self-confidence particularly when worn as a ring.

# Third Chakra

## Names

Manipuraka (Jewel of the Navel)
Lumbar Center
Solar Plexus Center

## Symbol

The triangle is pointing down, with swastika marks on the three sides. This is the fire wheel. This chakra is associated with the sun and the ego. It's also the center of digestion, which the Chinese call the triple warmer because heat is generated in the process of digestion. On the outside are ten lotus petals.

## Location

at the solar plexus (below the breastbone, behind the stomach) also shown at the navel

## Color

yellow
*Antidote*, violet

## Tone

a-o-m (ahh-ooo-mmm)
*Note*, e

## Element

fire

## Sense

sight

## Statement

"I want happiness"

## Explanation

The third chakra is the center of personal power. When the third chakra is open, you have found your own unique gift, the work that gives you pleasure and makes you feel fulfilled. When you're at the third chakra level of development, it's appropriate to build a positive self-image (ego). At the sixth chakra level you'll need to let go of your attachment to that image.

One way to find your gift is to consider what you most enjoyed doing when you were a child. This will give you clues about your natural inclinations. It's quite a joy to discover that what you're supposed to do is what you most deeply desire to do.

Your gift will reflect your natural skills and aptitudes, but it will also respond to training and schooling. For example, an opera singer is born with a beautiful voice but requires training to develop that skill. According to the yogic chakra system, the third chakra is also the center of intelligence.

In the martial arts the third chakra is considered the center of chi, the life force energy. So this chakra relates to physical abilities and athletic prowess.

Yellow is the color of happiness. As an example of how this works, when I was living in Seattle I was involved in an unhappy relationship when a psychic woman told me that I needed more yellow. One gloomy Seattle day, I had a terrible argument with this man, and I stomped out of the house and walked up the street.

As I was walking, I saw a whole rock face covered with beautiful yellow and orange flowers and I said to myself, "She said I need more yellow." So I proceeded to inhale the rich yellow as I gazed at these brilliant flowers. Within minutes, I was filled with joy.

After that I painted my desk yellow. I liked it so well that I painted my bookcase yellow. That was so pleasing that I painted my whole room yellow.

*The Book of Guidance* says, "You see my sun as yellow. Through the color yellow I give you warmth and an inner glow. I radiate. This is the source of relaxation. Deep relaxation. Because you relax when you feel accepted. Then you can stop trying so hard. When you come out to the beach and lie in the sun, you relax completely because you know that nothing is expected of you. When you know that nothing is expected of you, you can just relax and be yourself. Now there is a place at the center of your body called the solar plexus. Just as my sun radiates acceptance, warmth, and relaxation from the center of your universe, you can also radiate acceptance, warmth, and relaxation from the center of your being."

Dr. Laing says, "Yellow goes straight to the soul. It is the common man. Common as the daisy and the dandelion. This soul is accessible to everyone. It is not esoteric or occult; it is ordinary.

"It [yellow] is the Middle Way. The Controller and Regulator. The Center of Strength. It is our link with the great Central Sun. It receives the radiations of the heavens and sends tentacles down to earth. It is a source of heat and energy without over-stimulation. Nourishing like sunlight."

According to Paramahansa Yogananda this chakra is ruled by the conscious mind. It is active only while awake. However, it can be trained in introspective, creative thinking which will then provide access to and influence on the subconscious mind. This helps to explain the power of negative or positive thinking.

Dr. Laing says of people who are balanced at their third chakra, "Their personal will aligns with the Cosmic Will. These people are on their own path developing their intelligence and personal power, making unique contributions in the world."

When parents have specific goals for their children, this sets up a conflict in the child's will. The child will be torn between love for the parents, and the need to develop his or her own power. If the child is loyal to the parents' expectations, he or she will probably not find his or her own unique form of

creative expression. This is how people develop what appears to be a superiority complex. The superior attitude comes as a reflection of parental pride
in this person's achievements. But secretly, this person feels inferior because
he or she never had an opportunity to develop a true sense of self worth.

Dr. Laing explains that in a less developed person, yellow will be
mixed with red, indicating an obsession with accumulating things for one's
self. Personal power will be directed in a self-serving direction and will not
bring with it a sense of fulfillment.

"The third chakra relates to digestion," explains Laing. "A balance of
energy here causes good digestion. A lack of energy here leads to poor digestion. Yellow relates to relaxation at meals and the flow of juices; digestive
juices and bile, as well as adrenal and sexual hormones, all things that flow
and radiate. Not blood because that is red and of the first chakra. But it does
control dilation and constriction of the blood vessels.

"Since the third chakra rules both the digestion and the mind, it is difficult to think when too full or too hungry. But fasting will calm the mind unless there's a disorder here.

"Radiant relaxation comes from here. The solar plexus is the Center
of Breath." The diaphragm is located at the third chakra, so the color yellow
at the third chakra is helpful for someone who's not breathing deeply because
of tension or fear.

## Tarot Archetypes

There are two cards for the third chakra.

### The Emperor

This card is predominantly reddish orange and yellow. A feeling of
energy abounds, as the Emperor sits square at the center. He does not look at
us; he looks sideways directly into the sun. He exposes only the logical, left-
brain side of his head. There are swirls of energy on his robe, and bees and
atoms of energy around him. There is a ram at either side of his head. He holds
a staff (the head of which is a ram) in his huge hands. This man is powerful.

This card represents the fire element. The phoenix rises on his shield,
with the sun in the background. His protection is his fearlessness. Yet we know
he will protect the innocent because his banner is held by a lamb.

At the level of his solar plexus he holds a sphere which represents the
world. His energy is worldly. The Hebrew word is Tzaddi, which means fish-
hook. He will bring in the fish, he will achieve his goals. His strong legs are
crossed in the number four, representing impeccable organization, which
enables him to accomplish great things. The Emperor represents stability.

### The Sun

This is a card of joy and ecstasy. The sun shines upon all the signs of the zodiac. The fairies dance like butterflies upon the jade mountain, encircled by a ring of hearts. The rainbow surrounds the sun. This card joins the solar plexus and heart centers in unconditional love and radiance.

Our spirits awaken and we find our gift to share with the world. This is a card of fire, happiness, and energy. The Hebrew word is Resh, which means face. This card is open, honest, and outgoing.

## Balanced Energy in Third Chakra

*Characteristics*

outgoing
cheerful
have self-respect
respect others
have a strong sense of personal power
have found your gift

skillful
intelligent
relaxed
spontaneous
expressive
take on new challenges
enjoy physical activity
enjoy good food
spiritual expression could be
       Jewish
       Karma Yoga
       Tharavada Buddhism
sexual energy:
       care about your partner
       highest goal may be to have a simultaneous orgasm
       sense of responsibility toward mate and children
       uninhibited
       relaxed
       can show emotional warmth

*Example*

This man owns a large health food store and restaurant. He loves to cook and enjoys teaching nutrition. His employees find him easy to work with. He's self-disciplined, reliable, and flexible. He rarely uses a recipe, preferring to cook spontaneously. He derives great satisfaction from his work. He creates a pleasant, cheerful environment.

## Excessive Energy in Third Chakra

*Characteristics*

judgmental
workaholic
perfectionistic
overly intellectual
as employer: very demanding
as employee: resent authority
may need drugs to relax
superiority complex fluctuates with hidden inferiority complex
sexual energy
       demanding
       constantly testing your partner
       complain a lot about the relationship

can be very affectionate

may desire a lot of sexual activity, but rarely feel fulfilled

*Example*

This fellow is very talented, but cannot decide how to channel his energy. He's a science teacher, carpenter, and musician. His father was a physicist and encouraged him to choose a career in science. He's a good science teacher. He drives himself very hard, but he doesn't enjoy his work. He complains frequently about his life, his job, and his co-workers. He worries about money constantly, and makes long lists of how he'll spend it when he gets it. He has many fantasies about women, but when he's in a relationship he's critical and argumentative. He has a pot belly and indigestion.

## *Deficient Energy in Third Chakra*

*Characteristics*

depressed

lack confidence

worry about what others will think

confused

feel that others control your life

poor digestion

afraid of being alone

sexual energy:

insecure

need constant reassurance

jealous, distrustful

*Example*

This man is usually unemployed, though he's a skillful welder. He feels overwhelmed by life and can't seem to accomplish anything. He spends a lot of time smoking marijuana and hangs out at the local bar with his friends, most of whom also have deficient energy in their third chakras. His wife is a competent woman who supports him and tries to boost his ego. He's possessive of her and may become violent if he thinks she's interested in someone else. Yet he has affairs whenever he pleases.

## *Contraindications*

People with nervous conditions and hot, red conditions should limit their use of yellow light to approximately five to ten minutes.

### Glands and Organs Influenced by the Third Chakra

the diaphragm (& the breath)
adrenals
skin
digestive organs: stomach, duodenum, pancreas, gall bladder, liver

### Illnesses and Ailments to be Treated with Yellow

digestive difficulties
gas
food allergies
liver problems
diabetes
hypoglycemia
over-sexed
hypothyroid
gallstones
muscle cramps, spasms
mental and nervous exhaustion
depression
difficulty breathing

## Stones

### Citrine

The citrine is a yellow to amber crystal which resembles topaz, but it's formed closer to the earth's crust and it's more readily available. Citrine is quartz which derives its yellow tint from iron oxide. This stone will help you get in touch with your personal power and express your unique gift. It will help you relax, feel good about yourself, and exude warmth and approval toward yourself and others.

Citrine will aid your digestion by relaxing the organs that produce digestive juices. It will free up your breathing by relaxing your diaphragm. Place the citrine over your solar plexus, or use a citrine crystal or a tumbled stone to charge water. To relieve wheezing during the early phase of an asthma attack, place a small tumbled stone in your mouth, preferably under your tongue.

You can also use citrine to charge massage oil. This will give the oil an energy that will be beneficial to your skin, increasing circulation and making the skin more resilient. If your skin is too oily, put the stone in a clear glass bottle of witch hazel (available in drugstores) for a week and set it on the windowsill, shaking it once a day. Then you can remove the stone (optional) and dab your skin with charged witch hazel.

Citrine is excellent for all mental activities. When you have difficulty concentrating or when you feel heavy and overwhelmed by worry and responsibilities, lie down and place a citrine on your third eye and another one on your solar plexus for ten minutes while you breathe in yellow light. It will help you to relax and breathe freely. It will dispel negativity and give you a more positive outlook. This could be combined with the Crystal Energization.

I use citrine at the solar plexus during most treatments, because it helps people get in touch with their own power and feel balanced and steady.

Wear a citrine around your neck with the point downward to improve self-confidence and to feel more attuned with the cosmic powers. This will help you channel the gold light of cosmic power down to your own third chakra. It's a powerful stone for people who are trying to break a drug habit, since it helps them feel better about themselves and it strengthens the third chakra.

### Turquoise

This stone opens up the heavens to the one who uses it with conscious awareness. It blends the color of the heavens with the color of water. It's a stone of peace, harmony, and beauty, in perfect attunement with Spirit. It's good for those who are afraid of power, or who need to use power in a balanced way.

If you use a good quality turquoise, this will deepen your work and make it last longer.

Keep a large piece of turquoise in a room, as a steadying influence.

Turquoise is a fine stone to wear, especially set in silver, to maintain a sense of balance. If there are digestive problems, wear turquoise as a belt buckle, bracelet, or ring. This is a good stone to wear on a daily basis. It has the greatest effect upon the one who wears it: it will increase their vibratory and healing powers, and give them greater wisdom.

### Malachite

This is a rich green stone, with dark green lines that often form concentric patterns. The essence of malachite is joy. Its name means emotional purger. When used over the solar plexus, this stone has the power to dredge up buried emotional pain. When that pain is expressed, you can release the heavy weight of grief that you've been carrying, and this leads to joy.

The energy of joy is a whirling energy—similar to that which pervades each chakra. In a healthy person the chakras spin happily in a clockwise direction.

When the spiraling energy of joy bursts through the malachite it leave its mark in bulls-eye patterns. When the malachite is placed at the solar plexus and a piece of green jade is placed at the heart center and a double-terminated quartz crystal is placed between them, people may remember events that have been blocked for years. They may cry or scream. As these buried emotions are brought to the surface and released, a great weight is lifted and they soon feel renewed.

Malachite holds the rich vibrations of the earth in its two shades of green, allowing the earth to love and comfort you while you draw upon her strength. This helps you to feel strong enough to face your problems so you can release old pain.

Katrina Raphaell suggests using this stone for drawing out physical pain. The larger the stone, the more powerful, though the ones with bulls-eye patterns are particularly effective when you place the center of the concentric circles directly over the painful area. The stone should be as large as the area that is painful. For nausea or motion sickness place the malachite over your solar plexus.

After using this stone, cleanse it in the usual way, and then—if it's been working particularly hard—place it on a clear quartz crystal cluster to recharge it.

This beautiful stone is good to wear as jewelry if you want to get in touch with your emotions. But if you're already too emotional, avoid it on your overly emotional days.

# Fourth Chakra

## Names

Anahatha (Unbeaten)
Heart Center
Dorsal Center

## Symbol

Two triangles, one pointing up and the other down, represent balance. The heart is the center, with three chakras above and three below. The six pointed star, also known as the Star of David, symbolizes the awakening of spirituality while being firmly planted on the ground.

## Location

center of chest

## Color

green or pink
*Antidote*, none needed, since it's central and balanced

## Tone

a (as in ah)
*Note*, f#
The combined sounds of everything on earth compose a harmonic chord which is the keynote of our planet. It's the key of f (or f#), whose note becomes visible as green. This sound is good for quieting the mind.

## Element

air

## Sense

touch

## Statement

"I want to give and receive love."

## Explanation

The heart chakra is the center of compassion. When this chakra opens, you transcend the limits of your ego and identify with other people, plants, animals, all of life. This is the humanitarian center. When your heart chakra is open, you're likely to become involved with social causes. You'll care about things like saving whales and the planet earth. You may find yourself working in one of the helping professions and participating in meditations for peace.

The heart chakra is your most vulnerable place. When you're hurt in life and love, the first impulse is to close your heart and say, "I'll never let anyone do that to me again." Of course, when you build a wall around your heart, you're keeping yourself locked in. Every time you experience a death or a loss, you'll either go through a process of grieving, feeling all your feelings (especially anger and sadness), or you'll close off your heart and remain in a state of denial, becoming numb to pain as well as pleasure.

In fact, the majority of people have closed off their hearts—often at a very young age—which accounts for the alarming amount of apathy that exists in the world today.

A major part of healing—with color or crystals or counseling of any kind—is to mend the heart. Your heart is at the center of your body and when your heart energy flows, your whole being is full. Then you radiate love energy to everyone around you.

Green is the color of healing. Almost all the healing herbs are green. Since it's at the center of the spectrum, green is the most balanced color. When you feel tense, it's wonderfully relaxing to go for a drive in the country or sit in a meadow of green grass.

Green is nature's way of loving us. Nature is full of the healing colors of pink and green. *The Book of Guidance* says, "The pink of the sunrise and sunset, the green of the forests and grasses ... these are the colors of my love. Just inhale and bring these colors into your chest, and feel the depth of my love.

"Think of a rich green meadow, and as you draw in your breath, inhale the green of the grasses, directly into your heart."

Pink is the most powerful color for sending love to another person. When someone feels needy, you can mentally direct a ray of pink light in their direction and you'll notice an immediate change. One of my clients lived with a psychotic man who constantly fought with her. I advised her to send him pink light when he was irritable. The next time he harassed her, she sent him pink light and, to her amazement, he immediately stopped arguing.

I was once invited to talk to a group of midwives. Many of them had been seeing colored auras around the women and babies they delivered, and they wanted to understand what they were seeing. The following quote was taken from a lecture that Dr. Laing gave me in preparation for this talk.

"The first thing to talk about is pink. Pink is the color of health. Babies should be pink. Vaginas should be pink. Pink is the color of love and good health. It is the central color. It shows that everything is in good balance and that love is flowing.

"If babies are not nice and pink, then they are holding on to their past. And that will happen when they are not sure if they are well-loved. A midwife should urge the couple to take time every day just for loving each other and the baby.

"If a couple want to become pregnant, the woman should wear a pink heart around her neck, and the man should cut his hair very short in the back (though this need not be visible; the outer layers of hair may be long, if desired). The pink heart indicates the woman's willingness to give love. The man's hair indicates his willingness to make sacrifices."

There's a common affliction of fourth chakra people. Since most of them used to be third chakra people, they're often married to third chakra people. As their fourth chakra opens and they evolve spiritually, they no longer share the same values with their mates.

Since the male sexual organs are in the first chakra, the center of physical reality, men tend to be more physically active. This energy is readily transferred to the third chakra, which is the center of chi, the life force energy. Men adapt well to becoming third chakra achievers, though this is more difficult for women, who frequently suffer from a fear of their own power.

The female sexual organs are primarily in the second chakra, which is the seat of the emotions. This energy is readily transferred to the fourth chakra, the center of unconditional love.

The New Age Movement is basically a heart chakra phenomenon. This helps to explain why there are more than twice as many women involved in this movement. Many (third chakra) men feel threatened when their (fourth chakra) wives becoming involved in New Age activities. However, there can be compatibility between a person focused in their fourth chakra and a person who is focused in their third chakra, provided that both personalities are well balanced.

## *Tarot Archetype*

***The Empress*** *(The Mother)*

The Empress represents intuitive, feminine energy. She shows us only the right side of her face. Her blouse is pink with spiraling energy patterns. Her pants are green. She is surrounded by moons, and we know that emotions are welcome here.

Like the Emperor, she has the energy of the phoenix on her shield, but behind it is the moon and the circle (instead of the sun and fire). Her left arm and belt emphasize her womb and the fullness of her body. She is nurturing. This card symbolizes fertility and abundance. At her feet is a pink swan with a nest full of babies.

The Empress holds the lotus at her heart center. She is surrounded by swirls of blue, and birds perch near her head. She is Venus, the feminine, receptive, and magnetic. As Venus she represents unconditional love. She combines the mental, physical, and emotional.

The Hebrew letter for this card is Daleth, which means door-leaf, like the opening from (or to) the mother's womb.

## *Balanced Energy in Fourth Chakra*

***Characteristics***

    balanced
    compassionate
    empathetic
    humanitarian
    see the good in everyone
    desire to nurture others
    friendly, outgoing
    active in the community
    discriminating
    in touch with feelings
    spiritual expression could be
        Sufi
        Unity
        Bhakti Yoga
        Mahayana Buddhism
    sexual energy
        can surrender and merge in a love relationship
        desire a oneness of body, mind, and soul—and will feel lonely in a relationship that gives less than that
        will power becomes stronger, which makes it easier to wait for the right partner

highest goal is to experience Divine Bliss—a spiritual, emotional, physical sensation—while in the embrace
of your beloved

*Example*

This Sufi teacher lives in a huge house, surrounded by luxurious,
profuse flowers. She is perpetually housing, feeding, and comforting everyone
from beggars to saints. Children are drawn to her. She has endless friends and
overflows with energy and love. Her lover is both affectionate and spiritual.

## Excessive Energy in Fourth Chakra

*Characteristics*

demanding
overly critical
tense between the shoulder blades
possessive
moody
melodramatic
manic-depressive
use money to control people
the attitude of a martyr: "I've made so many sacrifices for you..."
sexual energy
a master of conditional love: "I'll love you *if...*"
withhold love to get the desired behavior: "You wouldn't do
that if you loved me."

*Example*

This man is a poet and actor. He's a passionate lover, full of emotions
rarely expressed except through his art. Outwardly he seems sincere and
devoted, but inwardly a fire rages and he can't control his moodiness, his
depressions, his grief, his fatigue. When he's alone he's miserable, and when
he's newly in love, he's ecstatic. But after awhile he becomes demanding and
controlling and he drives away the one he loves.

## Deficient Energy in Fourth Chakra

*Characteristics*

feel sorry for yourself
paranoid
indecisive
afraid of
letting go
being free

getting hurt
family members getting hurt
being abandoned
sexual energy
feel unworthy of love
can't reach out
terrified of rejection
need constant reassurance

*Example*

This is the woman who loves too much. Because she wasn't well loved as a child, she doesn't believe she's worthy of love. She may be attractive and competent, but she chooses a mate who resembles the father or mother who was unable to give her the love she craved. Her greatest desire is to change her mate into a loving person through the power of her love. She does everything for him, but she ends up trying to control him and he often resists by pushing her away.

## Contraindications

## Glands or Organs Influencedby the Fourth Chakra

heart
lungs
immune system
thymus gland
lymph glands

## Illnesses and Ailments to be Treated with Green or Pink

heart pain
heart attack
high blood pressure
negativity
fatigue
difficulty breathing
tension
insomnia
anger
paranoia
cancer

*NOTE:* The best color for treating cancer is green. Ordinarily white light can be used for any ailment, because it contains all the colors. However, white light is nourishing and should not be used for cancer, because it feeds the cancer. Green selects only the healthy cells to nourish.

## *Stones*

### *Green Jade*

When your heart feels threatened or frightened, jade is like a loving father, reaching out his hand to give comfort, reassurance, and protection. Place the jade directly on your heart when you're feeling weak and vulnerable. Jade is grounding and stable. It has a gentle strength, and it conveys that strength to the one who wears it.

Jade embodies the love of nature. It holds and gives warmth. It's soothing—especially smooth pieces of jade. I like to carry a piece of water-worn jade in my pocket and hold it in my hand; it's like holding hands with a friend. The stone becomes warm and comforting. After charging it in this way, it becomes a wonderful gift.

This is the favorite stone of the Chinese. They say it has wisdom, clarity, justice, courage and modesty. It gives you the wisdom to make clear judgments, the courage to follow through on them, and keeps you from getting big-headed about the good results.

Jade draws impurities from the body. Use it over swollen glands—in the neck, for example. The stone should be at least as large as the gland. Hold it over the gland for at least ten minutes, as often as needed. I've seen it reduce swellings by fifty percent in ten minutes.

Laeh Maggie Garfield, healer and author, recommends jade for broken bones and tooth problems. For bones, she tucks a small tumbled piece of jade just under the cast, and for teeth, she places a small tumbled piece of jade in the mouth, next to the painful tooth, which causes a beneficial vibration when you speak.

This is an excellent stone to wear on a daily basis. It holds the energy of green, which is perfectly balanced and healing. It's especially good as jewelry for public speakers and teachers. Light green jade, such as Chinese jade and jadeite, carries the energy of love and forgiveness. It will help you to gracefully accept that which is difficult. However, if you want to be firm and assertive, you'd do better to wear dark jade, such as B.C. jade (from British Columbia in Canada).

### *Rose Quartz*

This quartz derives its soft pink tint from titanium. It's the gentlest of stones, with a soothing vibration that penetrates the heart and brain, soothing away your worries. For those who've been hurt in love or who suffer from a broken heart, rose quartz is like the Divine Mother, the ultimate comforter, who rocks you in her arms and gives you unconditional love. I use this stone whenever someone says, "My heart hurts." Its gentle pink ray penetrates deep into the cracks of a wounded heart, soothing and giving comfort, enabling the pain to heal quickly. It works with the pink energy of love, helping you to love yourself.

Rose quartz has the ability to heal the child within. So whenever you're exploring childhood traumas, place at least one piece of rosy quartz at your heart. When you've been hurt in love, let rosy quartz comfort your heart.

Rose quartz will help you to love and nurture yourself, and to believe that you're worthy of love. I think of this stone as being like a cuddly little girl in a pink dress, glowing with unconditional love and affection.

Laeh Garfield recommends rose quartz for alcoholics. She says that carrying a decent-sized piece (about the size of a quarter) will take away the need to drink alcohol. Alcoholics frequently drink to numb the pain they feel from lack of love.

This is the stone for skeptics and for those who want to open to their own spirituality but are constantly having to do battle with an overdeveloped intellect that feels deeply threatened by the intuition. This may be another reason why it's a good stone for alcoholics; I believe that many alcoholics are highly sensitive, intuitive people who grew up in a society that laughed at their sensitivity. In order to dull their sensitivity, they numbed themselves with alcohol.

To draw the love energy up to your head, and to persuade your mind to accept your spirit, you can lie down and put the rose quartz on your third eye. When you're sitting and meditating, you can put it on top of your head.

### Aventurine

This light green quartz is a granular gemstone with a metallic glint. It's composed of sparkling particles which, when placed or worn near the heart, set up an energy that protects the heart from other people's negativity. There's a softness about this stone, which is midway between the jade and the rose quartz. It allows you to be soft and open without being overly vulnerable.

Aventurine is soothing to one who is just opening their heart, after having closed it down. It's best to have the smooth stone in direct contact with your skin, on your chest. If the stone is pointed, wear the point on top.

This is the stone of unlimited possibilities. It opens vast horizons. It's the stone of the dreamer. It brings pure joy, unfettered by limitations. Use aventurine when you feel too confined, too inhibited, unable to break out of narrow ways of thinking or outmoded behavior. It's excellent for young people going out on their own. It's comforting to women going back to work or school after raising their children.

89

Aventurine gives the energy of protection in a light-hearted way. It radiates love without being possessive. It liberates. It has energy and enthusiasm. Carry it in your pocket or wear it any time, to feel a connection with its high energy.

Aventurine has the power to soften the vibrations of people who have a hard exterior but are genuinely loving. It will help them to express their inner love in a way that is more pleasing to others.

This is definitely an uplifting stone, and it can be safely used by those who get depressed.

Aventurine makes a nice present. It radiates good cheer. It's delightful to wear as jewelry since it constantly gives out energy that nurtures the heart of the one who wears it as well as the heart of whoever beholds it.

### Watermelon Tourmaline

This beautiful green and pink stone creates even more vulnerability than the rose quartz. The green gives protection and comfort to the vulnerable pink. It's like being held in loving arms that are so comforting that you can no longer hold back your tears.

The vulnerability that surges up with this stone can be overwhelming. The mind melts and with it the walls that both protect and hold you prisoner.

A large piece or a cross-section slice of a large piece will help to open tunnels where you have shut down, toward another person, or toward aspects of yourself. Don't use this stone unless you're prepared to be truly naked.

Watermelon tourmaline is a valuable part of your armamentarium if you're doing crystal healings. Whenever a person's heart is closed off, if this person truly desires to open their heart, place this stone (even a small piece, if that's all you have) at the center of the heart chakra. You can surround it with rose quartz and jade and clear quartz crystals, to strengthen it. Allow these stones to remain on the heart chakra for at least ten minutes.

While you're doing this, encourage the person to speak freely about whatever comes to mind. You can reassure them that it's all right to cry or express whatever feelings may arise. Then wait quietly and patiently. There's no need to talk.

Another use of watermelon tourmaline is when you have to negotiate with someone who is rigid and intractable. Usually such people have a history of having been hurt by parents who were rigid and unloving toward them. Their rigidity is a form of protection. If they sense that you're not a threat to them, they may be willing to cooperate (though perhaps begrudgingly). You can prepare yourself for such a meeting by meditating and attuning to the energy of the watermelon tourmaline. Ask to become a vehicle for the energies of this stone. While you're with this person, put the stone in your pocket where you can touch it, or wear it as jewelry. It's advisable to also have an amethyst crystal with you, for protection. You'll probably find that this person will be more receptive to you and their heart will be less closed.

Don't wear this stone as jewelry unless you're prepared to be vulnerable.

# Fifth Chakra

## Name

Visshudha (Pure)
Cervical Center
Throat Center

## Symbol

The circle of unity with All That Is comes within the triangle, indicating an increasing openness to Spirit.

## Location

bottom of neck

## Color

blue
*Antidote*, red

## Tone

u (as in blue)
*Note*, g#

## Element

ether

## Sense

hearing

## Statement

"I want to speak freely and openly."

## Explanation

When you reach this level of spiritual development, you have to squeeze through a bottleneck. It's a struggle. Society doesn't require it of you—in fact, many people frown upon it. You can function perfectly well from your first three chakras. If you open your fourth, that's extraordinary. But to open your fifth is walking on thin ice. The majority of people in this Dwapara Yuga are functioning from their lower chakras and they can't understand the person who opens to their spirituality. It makes them uncomfortable.

Fortunately, people have become more open-minded since Shirley MacLaine went "out on a limb" about her interest in metaphysics, and since the cosmic energies intensified around the time of the Harmonic Convergence of August 16-17, 1987.

The fifth chakra is the center of communication, so there's a powerful desire to talk about what you're experiencing. When you do this, some of your old friends will fall away. Your true friends will always be there for you, so try to let go of the ones who are uncomfortable with the new person that you are becoming. You'll find that there are many new and wonderful friends who will be magnetically drawn to you as your own energy changes.

*The Book of Guidance* says, "Sit and inhale this color ... As you absorb blue into your being, you will experience a cool feeling, a calm feeling, a slowing down of your energies.

"Blue must be used with moderation. One can get so slow that one loses all motivation, all excitement, all appreciation of life force.

"But most people can do with more blue. There is a deficit of this calm energy in the world today. There is so much clamor for excitement, for the opposite red energy, because people have become numb inside .... So these people who crave stimulation do not often appreciate the calming energy of the blue.

"It is my quietness. It is my stillness. I fill my sky with it. I fill my waters with this wonderful color. It is one of my greatest gifts to you. Fishermen and swimmers and pilots often know the peace of going 'into the wild blue yonder.' It calls to them in a way they cannot explain.

"When you feel the blue, you experience my essence. You partake in divinity. You lose your ego consciousness and experience complete bliss."

Spiritual children are those who have not closed down their fifth chakra. Their parents allow them to speak freely, to sing, and when necessary, to cry and scream. They've been encouraged to trust their own perceptions and to follow their instincts.

These children may experience conflict when they enter school and encounter a new set of values. This often results in chronic sore throats or ear infections (which indicate an inability to speak freely or an unwillingness to hear what is being said to you). The blue light will comfort these children. They need to talk about the conflict they're feeling and be reassured that their reality—though it's different from the norm—is valid.

As an example of how blue can be used therapeutically, Dr. Laing gave the following instructions to a group of midwives: "If the baby's skin is too red, then it is too excited. This condition should be watched closely because it can become habitual and lead to heart troubles and high blood pressure in later life. If the baby's mother learns how to handle it, these patterns can be changed. Help the baby to relax. To do this, help the mother to relax. Impress upon her that her relaxation is good for the baby. Give her plenty of blue light. Put her under a blue lamp. Have her wear blue clothes. Listen to soothing music. Bring in blue flowers. Create a calm environment."

Later he said, "When children are too excited, use blue. Always have on hand a blue outfit. The reason why little boys are traditionally dressed in blue is because most boys have more energy, and this is a way of calming them down."

One of my students is a kindergarten teacher. After learning about the calming effect of blue, she instituted a new program for her children. On days when all the kids are climbing the walls, yelling and screaming and acting out, she'll say, "Today's a blue day!" Then she'll bring out blue poster paint and blue play dough and blue construction paper and blue magic markers and she'll tell each child to do a project in blue. She says the effect is remarkably calming. In fact, blue classrooms are used for hyperactive children and blue holding rooms are used in prisons.

Blue can also be used effectively for the dying. Blue pictures, blue blankets, and blue flowers are calming and soothing to one who is letting go of life. If you're sitting by the bedside of one who is dying, the tone "u" (as in blue) can help to calm their nerves and accompany them into a different reality. Try it, and see if the effect seems beneficial. Perhaps this person will want to join you. But do not persist if the sound isn't pleasing to them.

## *Tarot Archetype*

### *The Hierophant (The Teacher)*

A man in an orange robe faces us. His face looks like a statue of a Greek god. On his head is a papal hat. (In other decks this card is also called The Pope.) Around his head is white light in the shape of a five-petaled lotus outlined in red, surrounded by a snake. Next to his head, a dove flies downward. At his heart is the image of a child within a pentacle (a five-pointed star), and his whole body is enclosed within a larger pentacle of light. In front of him is a small blue image of the priestess. Behind him is a bull and an elephant. In the four corners of the card are faces representing the four cardinal signs of the zodiac.

The Hierophant is grounded. He is Taurus, the bull, and his robe flows down to the earth, yet he carries the Priestess within. She is mystical; she carries the sword of thought and the moon of receptivity. She is his inner voice.

The Hierophant is totally centered and calm as he channels all these forces through him. His eyes are sculpted without pupils; his focus is within. He is the Revealer of the Light, the one who brings heaven down to earth. He is the sage and the philosopher, and he teaches by speaking. His number is five, the pentacle, the symbol of the human being, with a head, two arms, and two legs. He understands the human condition.

The lotus of enlightenment is at his head. The dove indicates that he can quiet his thoughts in meditation. The snake indicates that he can raise the kundalini.

He holds the child in his heart, which shows that he remembers his past, embraces it, and is complete.

The Hebrew word is Vav, which means nail. The nail joins the beams which provide shelter. The Hierophant (or the Pope) joins, heals, and marries.

95

### *Balanced Energy in Fifth Chakra*

contented
centered
can live in the present
perfect sense of timing
good speaker
musically or artistically inspired
can meditate and experience Divine Energy
easy grasp of spiritual teachings
may be overwhelmingly prolific
spiritual expression could be
        Quaker
        Spiritualist Church
        Agni Yoga
        private worship
sexual energy

when all five chakras are open, can manifest incredible
sexual or sensual energy, or can abstain without
great effort

may choose to rechannel sexual energy into music, art or
meditation

may be interested in nonorgasmic Tantric forms of sexual
expression

may vacillate between seeking bliss through sexual embrace
and seeking bliss through celibacy and meditation

*Example*

This man is a popular writer, choosing unusual topics of a metaphysical nature just as the public becomes ready to read such material. He plays the
violin for pleasure. He's highly intuitive, living fully in the present, waiting
until everything feels right before making any moves. He is always at the right
place at the right time. He practices Tai Chi and meditation daily. He's devoted
to friends and family, though he sometimes goes off into the mountains for
weeks at a time. His wife shares his interest in combining spiritual and sexual
energies, and they're both sensual and uninhibited.

## Excessive Energy in Fifth Chakra

*Characteristics*

arrogant
self-righteous
talk too much
dogmatic
addictive
sexual energy
excessive sexual energy
may be unconsciously macho
prefer partners who can be dominated

*Example*

This therapist is a large, overbearing, bitter woman who has a lot of
anger toward men. She's an articulate champion of women's rights, and has
deep insights which make her a good therapist and writer. When she likes someone, she's a good friend, but when she turns against them, she's rude and
abusive. She attracts sexual partners who are submissive and meek.

## Deficient Energy in Fifth Chakra

*Characteristics*

scared, timid

97

hold back
quiet
inconsistent
unreliable
weak
devious, manipulative
can't express your thoughts
sexual energy
>can't relax
>feel conflict with your religious upbringing
>may be afraid of sex

*Example*

This fifty-five-year-old woman was once a lawyer, but she dropped out in order to follow her spiritual master. Sometimes she has deep insights, feelings of ecstasy, and experiences a profound love of Spirit. At other times she feels like a failure and a misfit. She's in conflict about her sexuality. She's nervous and worries a great deal. She lives in a communal house and doesn't fit in. She's afraid to express her needs openly so others consider her devious and manipulative.

## Contraindications

Don't use blue light for more than thirty minutes, or it may cause you to feel withdrawn or "blue," and sleepy. If this occurs, follow the treatment with a few,minutes of yellow or orange.

Do not use blue for the following ailments:
colds
muscle contractions
paralysis
poor circulation

## Glands and Organs Influenced by the Fifth Chakra

throat
thyroid
nerves
eyes
muscles

## Illnesses and Ailments to be Treated with Blue

Since virtually every illness is characterized by inflammation, which is a red condition, blue is the most frequently used color for healing. Use it to heal all hot, red, and nervous conditions. Use it as an antidote for irritations in the first chakra area.

hyperthyroid
sore throat
inflammations
burns
skin irritations, rashes
fever
ear infections
overtired
mentally exhausted
gum inflammation, teething
ulcers, digestive irritation
nervousness
colic
back pain
hemorrhoids
high blood pressure
toxemia of pregnancy
vaginal infections
hyperactive
excitable and violent
during the death watch

## Stones

### Sodalite

This deep blue stone often has flecks of white and resembles lapis, but it lacks the gold flecks of iron pyrite. When both stones are unpolished, the sodalite is shinier. This stone will give you a strong connection with spirit while keeping you grounded in reality.

Sodalite is invaluable for anyone having a bad trip, whether it's a bad drug experience or travel sickness or depression. Hold it to your third eye and sodalite will be your life preserver, bringing you gently back to shore. This stone is good for anyone who feels too spaced out.

Sodalite is soothing to the third eye when you've been doing a lot of psychic work. It can be placed directly over the third eye or worn anywhere on the body. I like to wear it as a ring, and will often stroke the stone, feeling its soothing properties while I look into the deep blue. It's also useful for deepening one's ability to concentrate.

Those who have difficulty putting their thoughts or feelings into words can wear or place the sodalite on or near their throat chakra, and they will be comforted and soothed, and they will relax, so the effort which caused strain will dissolve and the words will come forth effortlessly. This will be a gradual process, almost imperceptible at first, but through regular use, good results can be obtained.

Too often this chakra gets closed off because as a child you were not allowed to talk about your feelings nor to cry or scream. If you were withdrawn and unable to express yourself, begin by working with your heart chakra. If you were verbally repressed as a child, you were probably also emotionally repressed, and you had to close your heart because it hurt too much. If this is true, you'll need to release emotions blocking your heart energy. This will enable the energy to flow up to your throat and then you'll find it easier to express yourself.

Sodalite will soothe all ailments of the throat. It will help to reduce inflammations and swellings when used over any area of your body, provided that the stone is of at least equal size to the area that is inflamed or swollen.

This is a stone that can be worn safely and beneficially at all times. It's good to wear as jewelry if you want to keep your head in the clouds and your feet on the ground.

### *Azurite*

When used at the fifth chakra, this beautiful blue stone enables you to give voice to your thoughts and feelings, and enhances the experience and expression of your spirituality, filling you with the desire and the ability to speak about deep things. I like to use a rough piece of azurite (in natural form) at the throat during treatments because it helps to bring up buried, rough emotions. It stirs up the throat chakra and penetrates the voice box so that you're filled with the desire to speak.

When used at the third eye, this stone will help you to reach great depths of spirituality.

When your eyes are overstrained from too much driving or too much work on a computer, lie down and put one azurite on each eye. I put cabochons (polished ovals) of azurite on each closed eyelid, near the corners toward the nose. After fifteen to thirty minutes, the eyes feel rested. These stones can be used in the same location to increase insight, allowing you to look within to find the underlying emotional cause of physical disease.

Two pieces of azurite may also be used for easing menstrual cramps or for ovarian pains. Place one piece of azurite at each ovary. These are red conditions and they are antidoted by the blue of the azurite.

When azurite is combined with malachite (they're often found together, or two stones may be used) malachite brings up buried emotions and azurite helps you to describe what you're experiencing.

This stone makes beautiful jewelry. It can be worn as a necklace or earrings, to enhance spiritual awakening. It will keep you centered and articulate.

# Sixth Chakra

## Name

Ajna Chakra (Command)
Third Eye Center
Christ Consciousness Center

## Symbol

Suddenly the multiplicity of petals falls away and you are left with two huge petals. Through letting go of your attachment to the multiple distractions of the world you enter into a Divine relationship with Spirit. This is the center of I and Thou. The two petals represent the various forms of duality: the ego self and the spirit self, the reasoning and the intuitive minds, the pineal and the pituitary, the ida and the pingala, the masculine and the feminine. All dualities converge at this point. The triangle is the yoni or female energy and within it is the linga or male energy. The linga of the first chakra was black, whereas this linga is white. The linga of the first chakra was surrounded by a snake, coiled three-and-a-half times around it, symbolizing the sleeping kundalini energy at the base of the spine. Now the kundalini energy rises to the

sixth chakra; the snake uncoils and the sexual energy rises upward. The crescent moon of feminine receptivity embraces the circle above it. This circle is a golden dot which is the essence of spiritual energy. It represents being in your center. The quarter moon is an energy vortex symbolizing infinite potential.

## Location

Each of the chakras can be located at the back or the front of the body, along the spine. The sixth chakra is found at the base of the skull, at the medulla oblongata. Its location at the front of the head is between the eyebrows at the third eye.

## Color

indigo (a purplish blue)
Indigo is a combination of blue and red. Red is warm, so indigo is a way of calming without cooling or slowing.
*Antidote*
orange

## Tone

mm or OM (as in home)
The sound "o" represents the sun or third eye, and "m" represents the moon or medulla. OM unifies both sides. It also combines the "o" of the second chakra with the "m" of the sixth chakra. This tone dissolves dualities and creates unity. It brings the ego self into union with the Spirit self.
*Note*, high "a"

## Element

electrical or telepathic energy

## Sense

thought

## Statement

"I want to see clearly"

## *Explanation*

The third eye is the center of psychic powers and higher intuition. Through the power of the sixth chakra, you can receive guidance, channel, and tune into your Higher Self. This is the center that enables you to experience telepathy, astral travel, and past lives.

When this center is agitated, it often indicates that a person had early religious training that taught him or her to be afraid of the occult. Many cultures and religions have taboos against anything vaguely metaphysical. While it's true that so-called magical powers been severely misused throughout history, the same can be said for any kind of power, particularly political power. And it is political power, including the political power of the established churches, that has outlawed or defamed practitioners of the occult, usually for the simple reason that these people were attracting too many of the churches' clientele.

The irrational guilt and fear created by these taboos make it difficult for most people to get a clear perspective so they can judge for themselves whether a teaching is beneficial or not. First it's useful to make a distinction between black magic and white magic. The white magic is the art of harnessing natural energy for positive purposes. If you're in the presence of someone who practices white magic, you'll feel normal, or perhaps your energy will be enhanced. Black magic is the manipulation of energy for selfish purposes. When you're in the presence of someone who uses black magic, your energy may be temporarily boosted, but within a short time you'll feel drained.

The energy of the third eye is, unfortunately, accessible to all people regardless of their moral and ethical values. The ability to manipulate reality is an appealing skill for those who are power-hungry, and this includes many New Age gurus. So be discerning about who you accept as a spiritual teacher. If you feel at all distrustful about such a person, pay careful attention to your perceptions.

For many people the word guru has disturbing implications of blind obedience and hero worship, and this has been a damaging pattern that many followers of gurus have fallen into. But guru is just another word for spiritual teacher. If you're fortunate to find a spiritual teacher you can trust, who feels like an innately ethical person, this is a great blessing. A true spiritual teacher should be simply a person who has progressed further in their spiritual development than you have in yours. Ideally it will be someone who has opened their higher chakras and achieved self-realization. If this is your goal, then such a person can be a great help to you. In every field where we seek to gain knowledge, we look for a teacher who is more knowledgeable than ourselves. The same should apply to the field of spiritual development.

Before the third eye opens, you see through two eyes: you experience a duality between your normal self (your conscious mind, intellect, ego) and your higher self (your intuitive mind, or Spirit). When the third eye opens, these two images merge—like when you see a double image through the lens of a camera and then bring it into focus as a single unified image.

I don't believe in forcing yourself to shed your ego through self-denial. I believe in working with the ego until it recognizes that the fulfillment of its highest dreams is to be found through merging with the High Self and becoming One with the Divine. Then all the masks fall away: who you thought you were, who you thought you ought to be, who your parents wanted you to be. Suddenly you let go and your True Self shines forth. "I am what I am." There is no guilt, no need for illusion or pretense. You are totally in the present and you realize that you were there all along.

The pineal gland is an endocrine organ that has the essential structure of an eye. It's located in the central part of the brain, so it relates to both the sixth and the seventh chakras. It functions as a light receptor, and is believed to be responsible for ovulation occurring in response to the phases of the moon.

When the kundalini rises up the spine, it stimulates the pineal gland, which may explain the experience of seeing the Pure White Light. The third eye is the Christ consciousness center. Everyone can have Christ consciousness. Jesus said, "The light of the body is the eye: therefore when thine eye is single, thy whole body also is full of light; but when thine eye is evil, thy body also is full of darkness." *Luke* 11:34.

The yogis say that the pineal is the seat of memory, so when the kundalini rises this storehouse opens up and you become a witness to all your past lives, and you see into your future. You no longer require the veil of forgetfulness because you're no longer afraid of who you are—you have nothing to hide. You're flooded with compassion and forgiveness and unconditional love toward all of your selves in all of your lives and you see yourself in everyone and everything. You no longer have any karmic debts. You stand released from fear and guilt and when this occurs, you transcend the wheel of karma: you realize that it was only a reflection of your ego.

Thus you become a fully realized being. This is the meaning of self-realization. You merge with Spirit and you become the Spirit within yourself: you realize your full potential.

## *Tarot Archetypes*

Two cards describe this chakra.

### The Priestess

The Priestess is Diana, the Huntress. Her elegant bow and arrow cover her lower chakras. She is sensual, but her sensuality turns inward. The sign of eternity covers her closed eyes. She is preoccupied and must not be disturbed. In her raised hands she holds a web; hers is the power to maintain the grid, the web, of electrical and magnetic forces. In the Hopi legend, she is Spider Woman, the one who weaves creation. Below her are signs of unusual fertility: crystals, strange fruits and flowers. She gives birth to new ideas and realities.

The Priestess is not of this world. She is entirely blue and white,

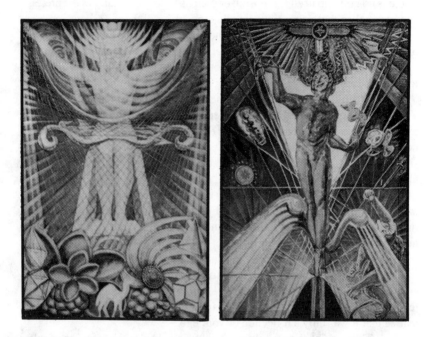

peaceful and pure. At her head, seven energy patterns arch upward. Spiritual energy swirls around her arms.

The Hebrew word is Gimel, which means camel, which represents self-sufficiency. The camel carries its own resources, it can go wherever it pleases, and it always has enough.

### The Magician

Though he is shown on the cross like Christ, his body is gold—the color of pure spirit—and he is blissful. He is a channel for the gods. He teaches by Being. He is the miracle worker: everything he touches turns to gold.

He holds the symbols of communication: the scroll for written words, the sword for the spoken word, the cup for feelings, and the wand for telepathic communication. He is Mercury, with wings at his heels. His message is the Word, and the Word is spirit.

The figure eight of eternity is seen in the snake, the caduceus at his head. The winged sun is another form of the lingam which represents the joy of life on all planes from the highest to the lowest. The bird flies downward, indicating that The Magician has no need for thoughts, he is in the realm of pure intuition.

Worldly forces (the monkey) approach him, but they have no power over him. He is grace. For him, all is love, all is one.

## Balanced Energy in Sixth Chakra

### Characteristics

charismatic
access to the Source of All Knowledge
can receive Guidance
experienced Cosmic Consciousness
not attached to material things
no fear of death
can show the way to liberation, through example
experience telepathy, astral travel, past lives
not preoccupied with fame or fortune or worldly things
master of yourself
spiritual energy could be
>Essene Christian
>Taoist
>Vajrayana Buddhist
>Raja Yoga

sexual energy
>At this level of development, you perceive yourself as essentially androgenous, and you no longer require another person to complete yourself. A partner who is needy distracts you from the bliss within. Thus celibacy is a natural choice at this point, but not a necessary one.

107

*Example*

Paramahansa Yogananda, author of *Autobiography of a Yogi*, was born to parents who were utterly devoted to Spirit. His birth was foreseen as that of a great teacher who would bring together East and West. Sexuality had no appeal for him; he embodied the essence of both male and female. He had no aspirations others than to serve Spirit.

Yogananda had the ability to heal and to make miracles happen, but he rarely showed off these remarkable talents. He had a direct link with Cosmic Knowledge, and could read minds, anticipate events, and see into the distant past and future. His predictions have been confirmed.

His charismatic personality drew swarms of people. He was in good health and of sound mind until his death, which he anticipated and which came peacefully. The morticians confirmed that no sign of deterioration was found for the three weeks that preceded his burial.

## Excessive Energy in Sixth Chakra

egomaniac
proud
manipulative
religiously dogmatic
authoritarian

*Example*

Hitler was a dynamic, dogmatic, charismatic leader with a powerful vision, who believed he could lead his nation into a glorious victory. His right hand man, Heinrich Himmler, was a zealous believer in the occult, which he used for his own demonic purposes. Hitler demanded total, unquestioning obedience and persecuted anyone who didn't follow his commands. He expected to be treated like a god.

## Deficient Energy in Sixth Chakra

*Characteristics*

non-assertive
undisciplined
oversensitive to the feelings of others
afraid of success
may be schizophrenic (unable to distinguish between ego self and
    Higher Self)

108

## Example

Sometimes this schizophrenic woman believes she is Joan of Arc, and will display dynamic strength and the ability to heal by touch and to foresee future events. Then she'11 sink back into a self-effacing personality, barely able to feed herself, afraid of everyone, distrustful, unable to find any direction in life.

## Contraindications

schizophrenic
withdrawn

Dr. Laing says, "Children do not need violet and indigo. These colors are too extreme for them, since they have just come from the Spirit World and are busy getting grounded. Still, some highly sensitive children will be comforted by purple when they're upset. The purple-flowered peppermint and catnip are, good for calming all children, and taking away nightmares."

## Glands and Organs Influenced by the Sixth Chakra

pineal
pituitary
brain
ears

## Illnesses and Ailments to be Treated with Indigo

pain (anesthetic effect)
diarrhea
agitation and tightness in intestines
psychic exhaustion

Dr. Laing says to use this color "like a bottle brush," to clean out the third eye when you've been doing a lot of psychic work.

## Stones

### Lapis

Lapis is a deep blue stone flecked with the gold of iron pyrite and it often has white streaks of calcite. It will take you deep within the vaults of your mind. This is not a stone to use frivolously; it may be dizzying for those who are highly sensitive to its powers.

Lapis was a favorite of the Egyptians. When placed on the third eye, it facilitates hypnosis, visualization, astral travel, and understanding of obscure religious teachings.

Lapis is beneficial to use during meditation. While sitting upright, place a piece of lapis (preferably a flat piece) on top of your head at the crown chakra. This causes the energies to rise and facilitates deep meditation.

The polished lapis helps you to put your spiritual life in the foreground where it will take on a sense of brilliant reality, while your normal life fades into obscurity. It allows you to step into your soul's natural royalty and don the robes of your higher self, shedding the rags of your ego self.

For someone who is already very spiritual, this stone may be too ethereal. Since it's such a powerful stone, it may make you feel dizzy or overwhelmed, particularly if you're being very cautious in your use of power.

When used consciously and sparingly, this stone has great power. But when used lightly, as in jewelry that's worn on a daily basis, one may become immune to its considerable power. Lapis is a stone to use with dignity and respect. If you honor its power it will compliment your own, and it will work with you to raise your energies and direct them for the highest good.

This is an excellent stone to use for ceremonial purposes, as jewelry or in a headdress or as inlays in temple walls or on your altar. Gaze upon its polished surface and allow its pure spiritual energy to come into your aura.

### Fluorite

According to Katrina Raphaell, this stone is not indigenous to earth. "It has been transported here from the higher dimensions." That isn't hard to believe when you look at the shape of this stone. It occurs in the form of perfect pyramids, octahedrons (which look like two pyramids joined together at their bases), and clusters. Fluorite occurs most commonly in four colors: blue, purple, white, and gold. Sometimes it's also found in pink and green.

### Fluorite Octahedron

The octahedron is the most common shape. When I asked this fluorite to speak to me it said, "I bring you the gift of Light. I can bring light into your brain as no other stone can do, because in reality I am crystallized light."

The six points of the octahedron make it appropriate for the sixth chakra. The points indicate that it will create a pointed focus and sharp thinking. Hold the fluorite whenever your thoughts are foggy or vague. When your mind is tired, do the Crystal Body Balancing and put an octahedron at your third eye. It's fine if you fall asleep with it on your forehead.

When you're emotionally upset and given to disturbing irrational thoughts, place a fluorite octahedron at your second or third chakra (whichever feels most distraught), or both, while doing the Crystal Body Balancing.

The purple, gold, blue and white fluorite in any shape will help your mind to integrate with your spirit, enabling you to accomplish unusual projects.

### Fluorite Cluster

These clusters are cubical in shape and they're usually purple. Raphaell says, "They represent the 21st century computer-age technological mind. Fluorite clusters are much like a computer and are very organized, structured, and complex. They look much like you would imagine an advanced space city to look, their cubical matrix displaying harmonious compatibility of all parts." She recommends placing them on desks, in laboratories or in places of study and research. Tune into them when the mind becomes tired, confused, or imbalanced. They help to keep the mind clear and focused even while working under tremendous pressure.

I've found that placing a cluster between and below the feet (while lying down), with one of the points between the legs (so that it has a diamond shape when looking down at it) works effectively to draw out negativity from the body.

I like to hold a fluorite cluster when I meditate. It grounds me and simultaneously attunes me to my spirituality. Since the fluorite is crystallized light, it reminds me that I too am a light being, even though I'm embodied in a form that's infinitely complex.

The cluster can be used as a key to the Akashic Records. Akasha is a Sanskrit word for the essence that holds the memory of all that has ever happened. It's a kind of cosmic library. So whenever you want to access this source of all knowledge, hold the fluorite cluster to your third eye, concentrate deeply on your question, and then wait for the understanding to come to you.

The cluster is wonderful for people who feel apprehensive about driving. It makes you feel organized, alert, and capable. Hold the cluster in your lap (to keep your hands free), or next to your solar plexus (for confidence), or next to your heart (for panic—like, when you miss your turnoff on the freeway).

### Sugilite (Luvulite)

This rich purple stone with streaks of black has just been discovered in the last decade. It's difficult to find and the price is high.

When I asked this stone to speak to me it said, "I can bring the energy of the Heavenly Father down to earth. I combine the purple of his robes with the black of the Earth Mother's caves. So my energy can course through your spine, from the top of your head to your base chakra—and into the wombs of women.

"Through me you become integrated. My spirituality can pervade every part of your body. As the energy of the garnet goes from the base to the crown, mine goes from the crown to the base.

"I am to be used and worn by highly spiritual people who are having difficulty living in their bodies. I will remind them why they came here.

"I am to be used by those with migraine headaches, by placing a small stone in the navel (directly upon the flesh) at the earliest symptoms, and then meditating deeply upon why they came here to earth.

"I am to be used by those whose life seems not worth living, by placing or wearing me at the heart chakra. Allow me to speak to your heart.

"Above all, I am to be used at the center of the brow where I can awaken the Christ Consciousness, where I can penetrate through to your Inner Cosmic Source and encourage it to open and shine forth to all who can receive it."

If you already sense what your gift is, the luvulite will help you to visualize ways of bringing that gift to the world, in a healthy and beneficial way. If you don't have a strong sense of your gift, you probably won't be drawn to this stone.

As Katrina Rafaell suggests, this is an ideal stone for highly sensitive children. It will help to protect them from the harshness of the world, reminding them that they're special and that their gift is rare and valuable. It will help them to feel good about staying in their bodies.

When discouragement and despair set in, place sugilite at the third eye, and breathe in its comforting energy. Remember that this stone came here recently, because people are becoming receptive to its special healing energies.

There is incredible power in a small piece of good quality sugilite (when the purple is rich and deep). It will help you to believe in yourself, particularly if you're small or extremely unique.

This is a wonderful stone to wear as jewelry, if you don't mind feeling as if you were on top of a mountain. You'll feel the wind whipping through your hair and you'll feel infused and inspired with confidence.

# Seventh Chakra

## Names

Sahasrara (Thousand)
Thousand-Petaled Lotus
Crown Chakra
Wisdom Chakra

## Symbol

The fully open lotus, the flower in fullest bloom, symbolizes being totally open to the Light. You've lost all individual identity and now you merge with All That Is. You become a fully realized being. This is self-realization, the peak experience of which is called samadhi.

## Location

crown of head

## Color

violet
*NOTE*: gold is also associated with the crown chakra.

*Antidote*, yellow

## Tone

ee (as in bee)
*Note*, high b

## Element

cosmic energy

## Sense

"seventh sense"

## Statement

"I want to be lazy."
(The seventh day is the day of rest.)

## Explanation

When a person enters the seventh chakra, there is a death. The person you were dies. Every layer of ego attachment falls away. You die to your old self. This Vajrayana Buddhist chant captures the mood perfectly:

Gone, gone, gone beyond
Gone utterly beyond —
Whoopee!

At the fifth chakra, you may long to leave your mark for posterity. At the sixth chakra, there is no more longing. It's enough simply to help by being a living example.

At the seventh chakra even the desire to help falls away though it may emerge again unpredictably. Now you become the divine madman or madwoman, utterly beyond laws and norms, totally unpredictable and unaccountable. Your behavior may be considered antisocial, amoral, and incomprehensible. But you are totally moral according to your own ethics.

You have the power to transmute matter into energy and energy into matter, which enables you to perform remarkable feats such as walking on water or appearing at several places at the same time. Food can be produced out of thin air. But then, you're a true breatharian—needing neither food nor water to survive. However, you're not likely to want to attract much attention, being neither a martyr, a saint, nor an egotist. So you're more likely to wander around in the Himalayas if you want to be left alone, or to wander from village to village as a mad storyteller, if you want to communicate in parables.

Your spirituality is omnipresent, and since you live constantly in The Light, there's no need for a path by which to get there, so there's no need for any organized religion.

Sexuality isn't likely to be desireable to you, though you may have evolved a form of energy exchange that's quite ecstatic and focused at any particular part of the body nor even to the physical body at all.

The seventh chakra is the point where the silver cord detaches from the body at the time of death. The silver cord is the fine line that allows us to astral travel and then return to the body. When this cord is severed, death sets in.

Death is no stranger to the seventh chakra person.

Since there is no separation between self and spirit-self, the body is a joke; a trick of the mind. Bodies come and go, but life is eternal. Since all the bodily cells can be transmuted and renewed, you're capable of immortality and you can perform miracuious healings and raise the dead.

## Tarot Archetype

### The Fool

From the outside he appears to be a clown. But The Fool displays the leap of faith—he trusts in the Universe. A lion bites at his leg, but he feels no pain since he embodies Everything. There are three interlocked circles around his neck. He understands all things, and his understanding forms a noose around his neck. It *could* be dangerous. (In other decks, The Fool has one foot off the edge of a cliff, oblivious to danger.) The fool has the horns of Pan. Pan is the God of Nature, whose name means all and everything.

The Fool is like the Buddhist monk who climbs the mountain, seeking enlightenment (fifth chakra). He reaches the top, fasts, meditates and finally attains Samadhi (sixth chakra). Then he goes down the mountain and gets drunk with the butchers (seventh chakra).

The fool has nothing to hide: he shows the soles of his feet. He is not grounded.

He has a breast, so he is androgynous. At the bottom of the card are the lovers of the second chakra. At the sides are the astrological coins and butterfly and in his left hand he holds the fire—all symbols of the third chakra. He has the green garb and grapes of the fourth chakra. In his right hand and on top of his head he has the crystal of the Priestess. Next to his head is the down-flying bird of the Priestess, Hierophant, and Magician. Like the Hierophant, he faces forward; he is totally open. Unlike the Hierophant, his eyes are open, glowing with inner illumination. He smiles.

115

He is forever young. He represents the beginning, the green of Spring. He lives totally in the present. The crystal light above his head indicates perfect clarity.

The Hebrew word is Aleph, another word for Prana, the breath of life.

## Balanced Energy in Seventh Chakra

### Characteristics
open to the Divine
miracle worker
can transcend the laws of nature
total access to the unconscious and the subconscious
ability to remain alert during and after death
almost immortal—or possibly immortal

### Example
Babaji appeared to Yogananda and to Yogananda's teacher, Sri Yukteswar, and to his teacher, Lahiri Mahasaya. He is always described as the eter-

nally youthful saint, who appears and disappears at will. Yogananda believed that he was one of the teachers of Jesus.

## *Excessive Energy in Seventh Chakra*

*Characteristics*

> constant sense of frustration
> unrealized power
> psychotic, depressed, or manic-depressive
> frequent migraine headaches
> destructive
> sexual expression
>> sometimes passionate, sometimes distant

*Example*

> This man had deep spiritual longings as a child. He grew up in New York City where he was expected to attend a Jewish Orthodox School. All students were required to wear tall black hats and black suits and to let their hair and sideburns grow long. He hated this school where he was told that God was cruel, demanding, and required strict obedience. When he graduated and left home, he became an atheist. He was often depressed. When his gloom became too overpowering, he would turn against his wife and friends. He suffered from severe migraine headaches.

## *Deficient Energy in Seventh Chakra*

> no spark of joy
> catatonic
> can't make decisions

*Example*

> This young boy never seemed quite normal, even as a baby. He was withdrawn, uncommunicative, and rarely smiled. When he was four years old, the doctors said he was catatonic. He was quite intelligent, but unable to relate to other people. He was pale and thin. Though his parents tried to love him, he was unable to respond. He was lost in a world of his own.

## *Glands and Organs Influenced by the Seventh Chakra*

> pituitary
> pineal
> nervous system
> brain

## Illnesses and Ailments to be Treated with Violet

depression
migraine headaches
parasites
black eyes
baldness, dandruff
*NOTE:* Violet is excellent for artists and high-strung, nervous people who need grounding but find red too harsh.

## Stones

### Amethyst

The violet or purple amethyst is the gentlest of stones yet it's a powerful protector. When you wear an amethyst or keep a large cluster in a room, it has the power to allow in only those energies that are harmonious to you and to deflect and transmute all negativity. It's the ideal stone to place on your altar.

The deep purple and very pale amethyst are the most powerful. Use amethyst over your third eye to facilitate visualization and past life recall. Hold the amethyst while you meditate, to calm and center your energies. If you have difficulty sleeping, hold the amethyst before going to sleep, and/or put it in your pillow. Or do the Crystal Energizing and simultaneously place an amethyst generator or cluster at the center of your forehead.

Since violet is in the red family, the amethyst is an energetic stone. While it's calming to most people, some children and those who are hyperactive may find it too stimulating.

This stone brings in the violet flame of transmutation, where the yang red energy changes to the yin blue energy. Yang and yin are Chinese words for extreme opposites. Chinese medicine teaches that whenever you have an excess of yang, it will change to its opposite, yin, and vice versa. Thus day eventually becomes night, and a fever can be broken by taking a hot bath. It's in this magical moment of change that miracles can happen, and that is the power of the amethyst.

Place an amethyst point or cluster on your third eye while you're lying down, or place it on your crown chakra when you sit to meditate. If there's anything that you want to get rid of, form a clear mental image of it. Visualize a violet flame in front of you. Exhale through your mouth and let your breath fan the violet flame. Inhale through your nose and gather in whatever you want to get rid of. Exhale through your mouth and feel that negativity going into the flame and being transmuted. Inhale through your nose while you draw in—

through the crown of your head—fresh new violet energy. Exhale and fix that energy at your crown chakra.

Amethyst is one of the finest stones to wear, because its energy is always beneficial and always protective. This stone should accompany any ceremony of protection and purity. It can be worn whenever you're among people who are hostile or potentially hostile. You can rest assured that only good energies will come to you and all negativity will be transmuted into pure energy and sent out into the cosmos.

### Clear Quartz Crystals

I place these crystals in the category of the seventh chakra because they capture the energy of the white light, and they're one of the most effective stones to use at the crown chakra.

The uses and varieties of clear quartz crystals are so extensive that I have devoted Part II of this book to these crystals.

# PART IV

---

## Instructions & Explanations

# Healing with Stones

## Definitions

In understanding the stones, it helps to have some definitions.

Rock: A large piece of stony material.

Stone: Earthy or mineral matter. I use this term to include all the healing stones.

Gem: A cut and polished stone.

Jewel: A precious stone, or a stone cut and polished for jewelry.

Precious: A gemstone of high commercial value because of its beauty, rarity, or hardness.

Quartz: A brilliant crystalline mineral made up of silicon dioxide. Includes clear and milky quartz, amethyst, rose quartz, aventurine, citrine, carnelian, tiger's eye, and agate.

Crystal: A clear, transparent quartz which is colorless or nearly so. Also a solidified form of a substance which has a regularly repeating arrangement of atoms resulting in natural external plane facets. This includes red garnet, smoky quartz, citrine, rose quartz, watermelon tourmaline, clear quartz crystal, fluorite, and amethyst.

Termination: A point where six sides of the crystal meet.

## Rough, Tumbled, and Gemstones

Stones may be either rough and in their natural form, or worked by humans in various ways. They may be tumbled in a rock tumbler, which is a process similar to being rolled around in a creek bed. They may be cut into various shapes to make jewel quality gemstones, the most common of which is the oval cabochon. The translucent (clear) stones may be faceted into shapes which are intended to make the stone catch the light more effectively. The tumbled or jewel quality gems are best for making tinctures and charging water, alcohol, or oil, since there are no particles to come out in the liquid. Gemstones and tumbled stones are good for smoothing over rough situations. Smooth, gem quality, and translucent stones help bring light into dark situations. On the other hand, rough stones penetrate to the depths, and bring buried feelings to the surface. Rough and smooth stones can be used interchangeably if you don't happen to have exactly the right kind of stone—both are effective.

There are human-tooled stones, made from natural crystal and other rocks. Some are designed with great skill, by artists who are like master sculptors, who can bring out the potential qualities of these stones. If one of these attracts you and you feel the energy is good, then get it. But it's a good idea to cleanse it carefully because it will hold the energy of the person who has worked it. Likewise, crystals decorated with silk thread, feathers, combinations of metal, and various designs should always be purified before using.

There are some attractive human-made gemstones, the most popular of which are German lead crystals. The clear ones are often placed in windows where they catch the sunlight in wonderful colored patterns. These colors are a joy to behold, and this is healing in itself. Lead crystals lack the depth of natural stones, though they derive power from their shapes and colors.

The best guideline when buying stones is that you should have a good feeling about them.

## Size of Stones

In most cases, the larger stones of any particular grouping are more powerful than the smaller ones. In other words, a large rose quartz is usually more powerful than a small rose quartz. Of course a small diamond can be more powerful than a large rose quartz.

But even within a particular grouping some small stones are unusually powerful. Deep rich colors bring greater intensity to a stone, as does a strong design. (In some cases, as with amethyst, pale colors also have a high value.) For example, the bulls-eye is inherent in the pattern of the malachite, and a small stone with a clearly defined bulls-eye is more powerful than a larger, less-defined stone.

## Basic Stone Kit

You can go to a rock shop and select the stones that appeal to you. Try to avoid pre-packaged kits because the process of selecting each stone will be the beginning of a meaningful relationship. As you work with the rocks, you'll find that you will remember exactly where you were when that rock came into your life. It's unlikely that anyone else can choose the healing rocks that will hold deep meaning for you (unless it's someone who knows and loves you).

When using stones for the first time, obtain at least one stone for each chakra, and four or five single terminated clear quartz crystals. This will give you the basic equipment to experiment with. As you read the personality descriptions for each chakra, you'll probably identify yourself. When you know which chakra(s) need work, you may want to get more than one stone for that chakra.

Start out with rough stones or small, inexpensive, tumbled stones. You'll find that even the small ones are quite powerful. Later, when you become more familiar with the stones, you can buy larger ones.

If you want to get seriously involved with crystal healing, here's a good kit.

1 long toning crystal (min. 2 in.)
1 channeling crystal
1 large single terminated clear quartz crystal
4 medium single terminated clear quartz crystals
1 double terminated clear quartz crystal
2 long thin delicate clear quartz crystals
2 single terminated smoky quartz crystals
2 garnets
2 obsidian
2 tiger's eyes
2 carnelian
2 citrine
2 turquoise
2 rose quartz
1 watermelon tourmaline
2 green jade
2 aventurine
1 lapis lazuli
1 azurite
2 sodalite
2 amethyst
2 fluorite octahedrons

*Explanation:*

In most cases, two stones are recommended because when you do a layout, you often use two stones on either side of a central stone. For example, if a person needs heart energy, you could put a rose quartz at the center and green jade on either side and aventurine on either side and long thin delicate crystals on either side. In some cases, I recommend only one stone, because these stones tend to be used at the center of the layouts.

## Stones as Jewelry

Another way to work with a stone is to wear it as jewelry. Lower chakra stones are best worn as bracelets, rings, or belt buckles. Fourth and fifth chakra stones may be worn as pendants over the heart or throat. Sixth and seventh chakra stones may be worn as earrings, nose rings, or tiaras. If you feel uncomfortable while wearing the stones, take them off.

## Stones in In Your Home

Enjoy the stones. Bring them into your life. Place them in every room, and on your altar, if you have one. Put them where your eyes will rest on them—including the bathroom. Put them near places where you often sit or sleep. Share them with your friends.

## Cleansing the Stones

When you use stones for healing or getting rid of negativity, it's a good idea to clean them. There are many elaborate methods of cleansing, but I find the simplest is to hold them under cold running tap water. Since energy follows water, the undesirable energy will wash down the drain. It's also a good idea to put your hands and wrists under cold running water.

Clear quartz crystals absorb a lot of energy, so it's especially important to do this with your crystals. Hold the crystal with the termination pointing downward, toward the drain. Each stone can be washed for fifteen to sixty seconds or longer, according to how hard they've had to work. If you're sensitive to their energy, you'll know when they're clean. If the water gets too cold for your hands, just set them in the sink, under the flow of the tap. If you're not sensitive to the energy, give each one about thirty seconds. If the work was very intense, give them a full minute.

When you receive a new crystal, or if your crystal has been doing especially difficult work, it's a good idea to bury it in sand or dirt or put it in salt water for one to three days. Salt water can be prepared by dissolving one tablespoon of sea salt in one quart of warm water. Or you can use ocean water. Keep a container of sand or dirt for burying your stones, and you can use it repeatedly, but change it periodically. For example, if you're using it for cleansing obsidian that's been used for intensive liver cleansing, you'd want to change it after about two weeks. If you only use it a couple times a month for special stones, you could keep the same sand, dirt, or water for three to six months. Arrange the stones so that there's at least one inch of space between each stone.

Another method is to smudge the stones with smoke from burning sage, cedar, or sweetgrass. These herbs have been used for centuries by American Indians for eliminating negative energies. This method is especially good for stones that are decorated with feathers or metal, or that are too large to hold under the water.

## Gifts and Ceremonies

When you have a stone that you love and carry with you or use frequently for meditation or healing, it holds your energy. This is one way of charging a stone. When it's charged with your energy it makes a wonderful gift to give to someone you love. If you've received such a gift, you can meditate while holding this stone and it will help you to feel the energy and the love of that person.

It also becomes a special stone to offer to the earth. The earth mother is constantly giving her gifts to us. It's a wonderful feeling to go to a place that feels holy and to offer to the Mother. This may be a place that you'll visit repeatedly. Or it may be a high and distant mountain that you'll never return to. Just knowing that a crystal you love is located in a special place is a way of feeling permanently connected to that place.

Crystals and other stones are wonderful to use for ceremonial purposes. A ceremony can be a special private meditation or a group gathering. It can be a full moon gathering or a celebration of the changing seasons at the equinox or solstice. It can be a world meditation for peace or for healing the earth. It can be a fire ceremony or water ceremony. It can be a special healing, or celebration for a newborn child, or saying goodbye to a friend who's going away, or to one who's dying.

Any ceremony will be enhanced through the use of crystals and other stones. They bring color, light, and beauty in a multitude of forms, and they constantly help us awaken to the beauty and abundance of nature and Spirit. Use them abundantly in any way you feel moved to.

## Altars

It's a wonderful feeling to set aside a place exclusively for meditation. It can be a corner of a room, or a closet, or a separate room. If you come to this place often and if your meditations are sincere and deep, this place will become infused with the vibrations of your meditations. You'll find that sitting here will fill you with peace.

Set up an altar in your meditation place by using a table or box. You can cover it with a cloth of a pleasing color. Decorate this altar with objects that are inspiring to you including crystals and stones, particularly those of the higher chakras. During your meditations, you may feel drawn to hold one of these crystals, or place one of the stones on top of your head.

It's good to represent each of the four elements at your altar: earth (a stone), water (a small bowl of water or piece of fruit), fire (a candle), and air (incense).

## Gemstone Tinctures

A gemstone tincture may be prepared by placing a stone in a bottle of vodka or some other form of alcohol. A small stone can be used to charge an ounce of liquid. Use a smooth or tumbled stone that doesn't have any particles that might come loose in the liquid. Ideally, use a gem quality stone that's been cut to reflect the optimum amount of light. Jewels that are set in rings or other settings can be used if they're clean and if you feel all right about drinking water that's been charged with that metal. Silver and gold are usually all right. Allow the stone to sit in the alcohol for seven days, preferably in a sunny window, shaking the bottle twice a day. Then remove the stone (which is still good to use for healing) and take 6-12 drops, 3 times a day, or as needed, to absorb the characteristics of that gemstone.

The same process can be used to charge water, which is another way of making colored water. It can also be used to charge rubbing alcohol or witch hazel (available in drugstores), both of which are used externally.

## Light Box with Crystal

To further enhance color and crystal healing, sit under a light box, and place a crystal inside the box, to amplify the healing and vibratory energies.

## Harvesting Crystals

With the current surge in popularity of the clear quartz crystals, the value of these stones has gone up over 200 percent in the last few years. These beautiful gifts of the earth mother are being ripped out with dynamite, thrown into huge trucks and sold at high prices.

There is another way. If you've ever had a crystal cluster, you may have had the sweet experience of having a crystal offer itself to you. When a crystal is ripe, it will loosen itself from the matrix like a loose tooth. It may fall off in your hand, or it may require a gentle twist to set it free.

There are people who mine crystals by hand, without dynamite. The crystals that are ripe are easily harvested. These people respect the earth mother and work with her like midwives. If you're fortune enough to find crystals and

other stones that have been harvested in this way, they'll be especially powerful for healing and for meditation.

# Color Healing

There are many ways to bring color into your life. You can absorb it as colored light; you can wear it as colored clothing or jewelry; you can ingest it as food or juice or colored water; you can take it in through your eyes; or you can visualize it through your inner vision.

In one of my workshops, a student asked, "How is it possible to receive the red ray from, for example, a red cloth—when we know scientifically that the red cloth absorbs the red ray and reflects back every vibration *except* the red vibration?"

Not knowing the answer to this question, I brought it to Dr. Laing. This was his reply:

"Let me start with an indirect explanation. In the beginning (as the Indian legends describe), the Creator Spirit created the four human races from the four colors of the earth: red, yellow, black, and white.

"This means that the red race, for example, would *contain* the red ray. They would not emit it; they would simply contain it. One would not receive the red ray from them, but if one were to rub shoulders with them, so to speak, one could receive—as if by osmosis—elements of the essence of the red ray. For example, the Indian culture is oriented to the earth—it is very grounded. By being in their presence, one can share in certain aspects of their culture.

"Similarly, the trees absorb the green ray and do not reflect it back to us. But by sitting in among the trees, we can receive, as if by osmosis, the essence of their color, and we can share in certain aspects of their culture, which contains the green vibration of love.

"But there are other ways of receiving the colors," he continued. "Through the nose, we can breathe the color into our bodies. And through the eyes, we can draw the color into ourselves. This is why can experience the color even in the dark, but it is more potent in the light."

There are several different systems for color healing. When you study other systems you'll find that different colors are used for the chakras. Try to find the system that feels most natural to you, and then stay with it. As long as you're consistent, it will probably work. I use the system I learned from Dr. Laing, which is based upon the progression of the colors through the rainbow.

## Colored Light

*Light Box*

     A light box may be constructed of hardwood or some other suitable material. It should be large enough for a floodlight to fit into. The bottom is constructed so that different colored plates of glass can be inserted and removed (see illustration).

     The box that is shown has three side boards; each is 8 by 11 inches. The fourth side, where the glass or plastic slides in and out at the bottom, is 8 by 9 inches. There is no board at the top; this is where the flood lamp clamps in. The bottom board is 6 by 8 inches with a 5 inch hole at the bottom that supports the glass and allows the light to shine through. The box which is illustrated is made of hardwood (otherwise this can be a potential fire hazard if the light is left on and the floodlight is too close to the side) and the wood is 3/4 inch thick (this is not necessary, though it gives a firm surface to clamp the light onto and to hang the chain from). The box hangs from a chain, which allows the weight to be adjusted and this is also fireproof. I'm sure this model can be improved upon.

     The lamp may be hung from the ceiling so that the light will shine through the glass onto the person who is seated below. Hang the box so the bottom is about six to twelve inches above the part of the body that you are treating.

     In deciding whether to use glass or plastic, there are several factors to consider. The goal of color healing is to strengthen and purify each color in your aura. According to many color practitioners, German glass gives the purest color and the highest vibratory intensity. In my experience, other kinds of glass are less than 80 percent as effective. Glass or strong plastic is needed if you want to put crystals inside your lamp. Glass can be obtained at places that sell stained glass. Thin plastic gels, by my experience, are less than 60 percent as effective as the German glass, but they are strong enough to give the beginner a feeling for color healing and they cost a fraction as much as the glass. Plastic gels can often be obtained at paint stores and theatre supply stores.

*Colored Lamp*

     A wire frame may be constructed around a floodlight. The frame is constructed so that it holds a plastic gel and the light shines through the plastic. The whole fixture can be clamped in a suitable place so that the light shines on the appropriate part of the body. These lamps are available in some health food stores.

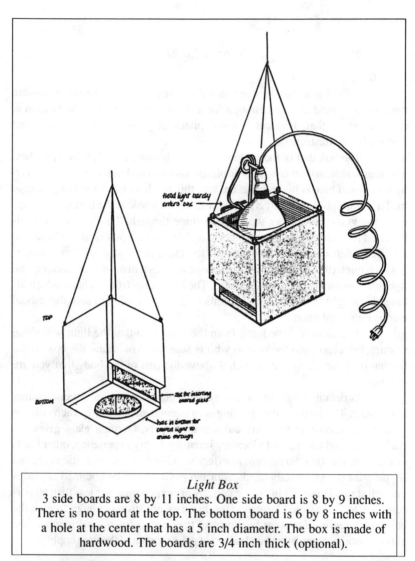

*flood light barely enters box*

TOP

BOTTOM

*Slot for inserting colored glass*

*hole in bottom for colored light to shine through*

*Light Box*
3 side boards are 8 by 11 inches. One side board is 8 by 9 inches.
There is no board at the top. The bottom board is 6 by 8 inches with
a hole at the center that has a 5 inch diameter. The box is made of
hardwood. The boards are 3/4 inch thick (optional).

### Colored Light Bulb

Ordinary light bulbs are often available in red, yellow, pink, green
and blue. They can be inserted into a regular lamp or light fixture. At night, or
in a darkened room, they will give off a good dose of colored light. Even
Christmas lights can be used, preferably all of one color.

### Stained Glass

The power of colored light was understood long ago, and may ac-
count for the popularity of stained glass windows in churches. Leonardo Da

132

Vinci wrote, "The power of meditation can be ten times greater under violet light falling through the stained glass window of a quiet church."

## *Fabric and Decor*

### *Clothing*

Given the opportunity, your mood will strongly affect your choice of clothes. When you understand the power of color, you can consciously alter your mood. For example, you may be feeling somber and withdrawn and be attracted to grey or black. But if you want to cheer yourself up, you would be wiser to wear orange, yellow, or pink. On the other hand, black is the color of mystery, so if you're in a pleasantly mysterious mood, don't hesitate to wear it. Grey is a neutral color; it doesn't commit you to any particular feeling, so if you're feeling withdrawn, it will leave you that way. But if you're feeling all right, it gives you the flexibility to move through different moods and to associate with various kinds of people.

The color of your underwear can have a strong effect on you. Red or orange underpants can stir up sexual feelings. Light blue underpants can be used to counteract nervous itching. Red or orange undershirts can cause tension in the back and should not be worn when you have back pain.

The color of clothing can also be used to create a particular impression on those who behold it. Deep purple robes are worn by royalty and high religious figures to create an impression of power and devotion.

On the other hand, bright red is often worn in the red light districts to give out the message of sexual availability.

### *Linen and Blankets*

A masseuse can use pink, green, or yellow sheets on the massage table to encourage clients to breathe deeply (all of these colors strengthen the lungs and the diaphragm). In bed, an erotic atmosphere can be created with orange sheets or blankets. A cheerful atmosphere can be enhanced with yellow.

On the other hand, a nervous or hyperactive child should never sleep with red or orange. A calming green or blue is most desirable.

### *Carpets and Drapes*

An argumentative family changed their wall-to-wall carpeting from orange to blue and they got along better after the change.

The operatic composer, Richard Wagner, composed spiritual music in a room with violet curtains.

### *Paint*

The color of a room or of furniture will certainly influence your mood and your health. Yellow cupboards in a kitchen will create a cheery atmosphere that's also good for digestion.

*Decorations*

Colorful decorations and paintings on the walls will raise the spirits. You can change them when your mood changes.

## *Nature*

Nature is full of color, and we can take advantage of her beauty and bring it into our lives. The way we landscape our homes and whether we live near trees or parks or water can have a profound effect on our well-being. Nature gives us a perfect balance of colors, allowing us to choose our favorite colors from her vast array.

*The Book of Guidance* says, "Think of a rich green meadow, and as you draw in your breath, inhale the green of the grasses, directly into your heart. In ancient times, people did this constantly and automatically. They looked into the expanse of blue sky, and they drew this color into their spirits. They looked at the yellow of the sun, and they drew this warmth into their place of happiness."

*Houseplants*

Colorful plants and green plants can be used indoors with pleasing results.

## *Visualization*

By visualizing color with the inner eye, you can use your third eye awareness to take in color. Close your eyes and get a picture of a color. If it's difficult for you to get a picture of yellow, try to imagine a lemon. When you see the lemon, let it fade and just try to see yellow. Color visualization is most effective when combined with color breathing, as described below.

## *Color Breathing*

The first three colors (red, orange and yellow) are associated with the earth. Think of these colors as arching up from the earth like a rainbow, and entering each of the corresponding chakras (first, second and third). The heart chakra at your chest has two colors: pink and green. Think of one of these colors coming directly across the horizon, toward your heart. The top three colors (blue, indigo and violet) are associated with the heavens. Think of each of these colors as arching down from the heavens like inverted rainbows, entering at each corresponding chakra.

If you want to visualize yellow at your third chakra, you could begin by getting a clear mental picture of a lemon, or the sun. Then inhale and visualize a band of this color arching up from the earth and flowing into your solar plexus (below your breast bone). As you exhale, fix it there.

If you want to send that color to someone else, always begin by breathing in the color and fixing it at your own chakra. When you feel that you have enough, you can send it. The third and sixth chakras are both power centers, so they are good transmitting stations. The lower three colors are usually sent through the third chakra at the solar plexus, pink and green are sent directly from the heart, and the top three colors are sent through the third eye. For example, if you're sending orange, inhale and bring the color to your second chakra (which is orange). Exhale and fix it there. Repeat this several times until you feel you have enough orange. When you're ready to send the color, inhale and this time bring the orange to the surface of your solar plexus (this time you're not trying to absorb it), and then exhale and direct it like a beam of light to the person who needs the color. Send it to the appropriate part of their body. As you exhale, you can also tone, which gives additional vibratory energy. Repeat this process about three times, and then ask the person you're working on how it feels. If the results are good, continue until the person feels that she or he has had enough (usually six to twelve times). If there is no significant response after six times, it probably is not what that person needs. The duration of a treatment should be determined by a combination of your own intuition and the response you receive from the person you're working on. If the person actually feels worse, it's usually best to discontinue the treatment though occasionally the problem will get worse, very briefly, before it gets better. But if it gets worse and does not get better after a few breaths, then give the antidote.

Color visualization can be done in the presence of the person you are sending it to, or in their absence. The same technique can be used for distant healing but instead of directing the color to a person who is directly in front of you, visualize the person in your mind and direct the color to that visual image or to a photograph or drawing of that person. This is a remarkably effective form of healing, because color healing is energy healing, and energy does not require person's physical presence. If you doubt this, then try it yourself—but have an open mind.

When you send color healing (or any form of energy) to another person, it is best to get their permission first. Not everyone wants to be healed, nor even to feel good.

However, there are exceptions to this guideline. If a person is unconscious or unable to speak or too young to communicate, then it's fine to send them healing energy if it feels right to do that.

Another exception pertains to using pink light for self defence. Pink light is extremely potent. Pink is the energy of love, and when you send pink light in earnest, you must be able to love (and, if necessary, to forgive) the person you're sending it to. If a person is being belligerent, irrational, or irritable, it's a powerful form of self-defence to send pink light to them. As soon as they feel the ray of love and forgiveness, they are likely to change their behavior. This may be an invasion of their privacy, but other forms of self defense would be far more invasive.

For example, one of my students was working at a health food store and a fellow came in who had had too much to drink. He was being generally obnoxious, insulting the customers and knocking boxes off the shelves. When she asked the man to leave, he ignored her. She was about to phone the police when she remembered the pink light.

Despite his behavior she was able to feel compassion toward this man, and she sent him a strong wave of pink light directly from her heart. Within a minute, the man picked up the boxes from the floor, apologized for his behavior, and walked out of the store.

## *Food and Drink*

*Color of Foods*

In Oriental cooking, the cook often strives to include the four basic colors. When a meal looks appetizing, it is pleasant to eat and easier to digest. A meal that contains the colors of the first four chakras will usually be nutritionally balanced. For example, a meal with tomatoes, carrots, corn and steamed greens would be pleasant and nutritious. It's good practice to steam the greens just until the color is at its brightest; when the greens darken, the flavor and nutrition diminishes.

The color of a food will often tell which parts of the body it will heal. For example, the first chakra is red, and it relates to the blood. Most of the blood-cleansing foods (foods that tone up the liver and lymph glands, enabling them to clean out toxins from the blood) are in the red family: red cabbage, cherries, cranberries, blackberries, and red clover tea.

When the emphasis is on the liver and gall bladder, we look toward the yellow foods. Olive oil and lemon juice make an excellent flush for these organs. Dandelion root tea is very strengthening to the liver and gall bladder.

*Color-Charged Water*

Water can be "charged" with a particular color, and then taken internally or externally. For example, the color of the second chakra is orange, and this chakra is in the area of the large intestines. If there is constipation, it's beneficial to take a few sips of orange-colored water (ambero) before each meal.

When I first heard about color-charged water, I found it hard to believe. The water doesn't *look* any different after it has been charged. But I'm open-minded, so when I got constipated, I decided to give it a try. I couldn't

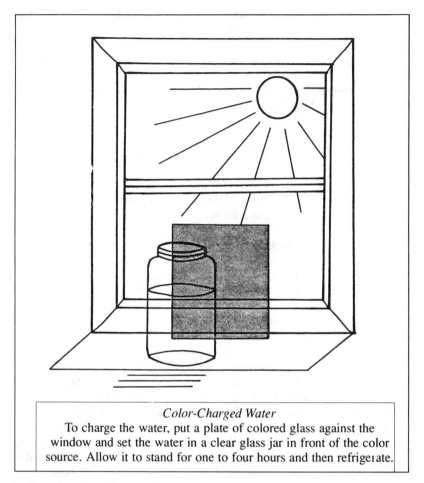

*Color-Charged Water*
To charge the water, put a plate of colored glass against the window and set the water in a clear glass jar in front of the color source. Allow it to stand for one to four hours and then refrigerate.

believe that a few sips would make any difference, so I drank about half a glass before each meal. By evening, I had diarrhea! Since then, I've taken the color-charged water more seriously. It has proved effective for many ailments.

To charge the water, put it in a colored bottle or jar (for example, a green wine bottle or a blue Noxzema jar) and set it on a windowsill so that the light will shine through the glass and into the water. Or put a plate of colored glass or plastic or thin cloth against the window and set the water in a clear glass jar or bottle in front of the color source. Allow it to stand for one to four hours (four hours will be stronger) and then refrigerate. Take as directed.

In cool weather or when refrigerated, red, orange and yellow charged water will last two to three weeks. In warm weather, without refrigeration it will lose its charge after three or four days. The other colors will last indefinitely. In fact, green, blue, or purple jars are used to help preserve oils, herbs, etc.

The French word for water is eau, pronounced "o." The following names are used for colored waters:
   red: rubio
   orange and yellow: ambero
   green: verdio
   blue: ceruleo
   indigo and violet: purpuro

## *Color Healing for the Face*

The face is a microcosm of the body, and Dr. Laing explains that the same colors that are used to treat the seven chakras can be used to treat the seven areas of the face, as follows:

1. Red: chin, jaw, lips
2. Orange: inside of mouth, gums, tongue
3. Yellow: throat, leading into intestinal tract
4. Green: nose, leading into respiratory tract
5. Blue: eyes, which are windows to the soul
6. Indigo: ears and third eye
7. Violet: crown chakra

Here are some examples of how to apply this information:
During their forties most people experience a waning of sexual energy (second chakra). During this time there is often a deterioration of the gums. This can be treated with a tincture made from pot marigold (an orange flower) or by rinsing the mouth with ambero (orange charged water).

When the eyes are overstrained, which occurs when you work too hard and don't take enough time for sleep and meditation, the fifth chakra suffers. This condition responds well to placing a cabochon of blue azurite over each eye.

# *Developing Your Intuition*

Healing with color and crystals is not intellectual work. You can read this book and learn the techniques, but that's like learning scales in music. You can learn all the scales and you can even learn to read music, but you won't be able to make beautiful music until you can play from your heart. Or your soul.

If you want to heal with color and crystals, the most important tool is your intuition. There are two kinds of intuition. The first kind comes from the second chakra (and, to some degree, the third). It's a gut-level-kind-of intuition. This is the intuition that functions when you say things like, "I can't explain it, but I've got a feeling that..." or "I know it's going to rain. I can feel it in my bones."

The second kind of intuition comes from the sixth chakra, and it's what we call the seventh sense, higher knowledge, the ability to listen to the inner voice. When you can access this higher intuition on a regular basis, your life will change: You'll always know what to do and you'll always be at the right place at the right time.

As you develop this ability, you'll probably find that healing with color and crystals will come naturally to you. You'll feel drawn to particular colors or stones, for yourself and for others. You'll have a feeling that a particular stone should go at a certain place, or that it should be used for a certain ailment.

The best way to develop this higher intuition is to start out by paying attention to your instincts. Whenever you have a "feeling" that you should take your umbrella, or that you should call your mother, or that you should stop at your friend's house on the way to work ... do it! It doesn't matter how irrational it may seem. Do it anyway.

Keep a chart. (See Illustration.) Keep track of every time you have a feeling about something. Write down whether or not you followed that feeling and the results. Then check either "Positive" or "Negative." If you followed your intuition and you're glad you did, count this as positive. If you didn't follow your intuition and you wish you had, count this as positive. Positive points indicate a positive vote for following your intuition. If you did follow your intuition and you wish you hadn't, count this as negative. If you didn't follow your intuition and you're glad you didn't, this is also a negative. Negative points indicate a negative vote for following your intuition.

Judging from the results that most of my clients and students have had with this technique, I predict that nine out of ten times when you follow your intuition, you'll be glad you did. And nine out of ten times when you

| DATE | FEELING | FOLLOW THROUGH | RESULTS | POS. | NEG. |
|------|---------|----------------|---------|------|------|
| 10/12 | take umbrella | I didn't | it rained, got wet. | ✓ | |
| 10/25 | drive to next town to buy shoes on sale | I did | they weren't on sale, wasted gas & time. | | ✓ |
| 10/30 | stop off on the way home, buy extra groceries | I did | husband brought friends from work home for dinner | ✓ | |

*Intuition Chart*

didn't follow it, you'll wish you had (though certainly some people have better odds than others).

The times you guess wrong will occur more often in the beginning because you're liable to confuse an intuitive thought with a wishful, fearful, or guilty thought. You might not know whether the urge to call your mother is coming from an inner knowing that she needs your help, or from a nagging sense of guilt that you ought to call her. (What we call conscience is *NOT* intuition.)

Until you learn to make these subtle distinctions (and it's just a matter of time, though you'll probably never get it one hundred percent right), you simply have to put up with a slight margin of error. But be careful. Your intellect is accustomed to being in charge and is liable to feel threatened when you begin giving power to your intuition. Your intellect is liable to pounce upon that one or two out of ten times and say "Aha! I told you so! You can't trust yourself!"

However, when you think about it, eight or nine times out of ten is pretty good. If your intellect could do that, it would consider itself brilliant. One thing you can say for the intellect is that it's reasonable. That's why you need the chart. Then you can calmly point out that the odds are good.

The next thing the intellect needs is a nice easy chair. It's been working too hard. Help it to relax and realize that it doesn't have to be in charge all the time. The metaphor I like to use is the difference between hierarchical and tribal government. Hierarchical government has one person in charge, whereas tribal government usually has a group of people in charge: the war chief, the chief of agriculture, the medicine man or woman, and so forth.

Body, mind, heart and intuition function much better in the tribal mode. Once the mind understands this, it will often cooperate and allow the body, heart and spirit to take over when it's appropriate. One of my clients did extensive work on this and then announced that his intuition was going to make the decisions and his intellect would implement them. This is an intelligent way to proceed.

# Meditation and Channeling

*Meditation*

Meditation is a form of private devotion in which the mind con-centrates on a particular practice which frees it from its normal thoughts. Most meditation techniques deepen and slow the breathing, which in turn slows the heart, which then allows the body to relax, which helps the mind to relax.

The ultimate goal of meditation is a state of mystical awareness in which you temporarily lose self-identity and merge with All That Is. With prac-tice, you may be able to achieve this by simply sitting down, closing your eyes and going within.

*Channeling*

A channel is a person who receives messages from Spirit, from her or his inner voice or Higher Self, from a spirit guide, from a plant or a rock. The process of doing this is called channeling.

This used to be a rare skill, but as more and more people are opening their higher chakras, it's becoming increasingly common. Channeling has to pass through the vehicle of the channel: it will take on the characteristics of this person, just as water takes on the flavor of whatever substance it flows through or is blended with. The messages received will only be as reliable as the combination of the person who receives them and the agent that sends them.

When you become adept at channeling, you simply go into a medita-tive state, quiet your conscious mind, tune in, and be still. If you have a specific question, ask it, make your mind blank, and wait for an answer.

But when you're just developing this skill it helps to follow a medita-tion ritual. There are many ways to do this. The following guideline will help you to achieve your goal. Follow all these instructions or only some of them. Don't hesitate to modify them to suit your needs.

## Health

When you're ill, you become preoccupied with your body and your energy doesn't flow smoothly. Take care of your body; it's the temple of your spirit. Always remember to get ample sleep, good food, fresh air, and exercise.

## Exercise

Begin by doing about fifteen minutes of yoga asanas or Tai Chi or stretching exercises to awaken your energy and calm your body.

142

## Power Objects

Sit in front of an altar or in a quiet place. A place outdoors in nature is fine, if you won't be disturbed. Surround yourself with objects that have good energy: favorite crystals, amethysts, well-loved stones, or photographs of those who have inspired you.

On your head place an amethyst, fluorite, lapis, or clear quartz crystal. In your hand (usually your left hand) hold a channeling crystal or your favorite meditation crystal.

## Incense

An odor which is pleasing to you may be used, such as incense, or sage, cedar, sweetgrass. These have a cleansing effect on the vibratory energy.

## Seven Colors

On the wall or on your altar, have each of the seven colors in shades that are pleasing to you. These may be frames to photographs, flowers, an altar cloth, a wall hanging, candles, or stones. For example, you could have each of the following stones on your altar: garnet (red), carnelian (orange), citrine (yellow), jade (green), sodalite (blue), lapis (indigo), and amethyst (violet).

## Posture

Sit cross-legged on the floor with your spine straight, or sit on a straight-back chair with your feet on the ground and your spine straight, not touching the back of the chair. Place your hands on your thighs, palms upward, and join your thumbs to your index fingers,and bring the tip of your tongue to the roof of your mouth to complete the acupuncture meridian circuits.

*Procedure*

1. With eyes open, deeply inhale each of the seven colors, from red to violet. As you exhale, make the tone of that chakra. The tones are described in each chakra section.

2. Do the Microcosmic Orbit, as described in Mantak Chia's books. The following is a brief summary of the method, combined with my own suggestions.

There are two major energy channels (acupuncture meridians).

The Yin Channel (the Conception Vessel) begins at the perineum and goes up the front center of the body and ends at the tip of the tongue.

The Yang Channel (the Governing Vessel) begins at the perineum and goes up the back center of the body, over the head and back down to the roof of the mouth.

The tongue connects these two currents when touched to the highest point of the roof of the mouth.

An easy way to open this energy channel is to sit in meditation and relax. Allow your energy to complete the loop by letting your mind flow along with it. Start in the eyes and mentally circulate your attention with the energy Eventually the current will begin to feel warm in some places as it loops around. Just relax and try to bring your mind directly into the part of the loop being focused on. Experience the actual feeling of the flow of chi in that part of your body. Once the orbit is going smoothly, inhale as you go up the spine and over to the third eye, and exhale as you go down from the third eye to the perineum (the area between the anus and the vagina—or the scrotum).

Count on the joints of your fingers as you complete each orbit. Do seven to fourteen. (Seven is a mystical number, partly because of the seven chakras.)

3. Bring the energy up your spine as you inhale, and send it up to the heavens. With it send thanks for all the things you're grateful for.

4. Imagine an overcast day. The clouds part slightly and a ray of light comes through and settles directly on your head. Absorb that sunlight into your being and with that sunlight bring in the blessings that are meant for you. Feel good energy coursing through your body.

5. Sit with that energy. Bask in it. Focus on your third eye and feel your connection with Spirit. Stay with this energy for as long as it feels good—at least five minutes.

6. When the highly charged feeling begins to subside, bring the seven-sided face of your channeling crystal, if you have one, to your third eye, or just direct your focus to your third eye.

7. If this is a morning meditation, you may wish to ask for guidance about the day. If you have a specific question, formulate it very clearly.

8. Be still and wait for an answer. If necessary, tell your conscious mind to step aside. Breathe deeply.

9. When you receive an answer, give thanks. Always give thanks. Focus on your gratitude toward the Spirit that has answered your question, instead of getting caught up in thinking about how wonderful you are because you can do such a thing.

(Even if this source is your own Higher Self, it's good to make this distinction between your High Self and your ego self.)

10. Write down the answer.

# Toning

Toning refers to making sounds which vibrate the chakras, awakening their energies. It can also be used to break up energy blockages, which are often the cause of illness. Each chakra has a corresponding tone which can be used to vibrate that chakra.

There are different systems for toning. In the section for each chakra I've given the sounds I find most effective. Each tone has a note on the scale—you can use a tuning fork or a musical instrument to find the note.

You can tone for yourself and derive great benefit from using your voice to vibrate your chakras. You can tone for and with other people to vibrate and open their chakras. To enhance the vibratory effect of toning, hold a toning crystal in your hand while you tone.

During a crystal treatment, if you feel that a particular chakra needs more energy, you can place a single terminated clear quartz crystal over the chakra, with the termination pointing towards the person's head, and make the tone for that chakra. Repeat the tone at least three times and then ask the person whether he or she wants you to continue. If the effect is favorable, repeat the tone approximately six to twelve times.

Begin by trying the tones I've given in this book. When toning for yourself place your fingertips lightly over each chakra. Experiment and try different sounds on different notes. Do this until you feel a vibration at that energy center. You don't have to be musically inclined to be good at toning. People who have no ear for music can be effective at toning.

Another method is to allow vibratory sounds to come out spontaneously, without regard for any chakras or systems. The notes and tones that I have given are just guidelines. Any note or tone can be used at any part of the body. Your best guide is your intuition.

Tones can be used to enhance meditation, to release emotions or to clear the air. Just making sounds will help to open up your fifth chakra, which is your center of spirituality and communication.

When I do the Crystal Balancing and Toning, I seldom use the tones that correspond to the chakras. Sometimes the sounds that come out are sounds of pain, or high-pitched shrieks, or low groans and moans. If I feel the impulse to make a sound, I'll usually warn the person I'm working on, and then I'll make the sound. If it feels like it's going to be a harsh sound, I'll ask permission to make it.

Your best way to judge the effects of your tones is by asking for feedback. If your tones are effective, your friends or clients will express their appreciation.

Sometimes when I make a tone, I'll get an image with the sound. For example, I was working on one woman's left knee, and I felt like moaning. When I moaned, it made me feel like an old woman. I asked her if she felt close to an elderly women who had a pain in her left knee. She was taken aback. Recently she'd been visiting an elderly woman who had severe arthritis in her left knee, who often bent over and moaned like that.

I knew this wasn't likely to make a deep impression on her unless it related to an earlier experience that was emotionally charged. I urged her to think back and see if there was another elderly woman, perhaps in her childhood, who had a pain in her left knee.

"My God!" she exclaimed. "I totally forgot! When my mother was dying of cancer, she often had pains in her left leg, and when we went for walks together, sometimes she'd lean over and moan like that."

Though there had been no pain in my client's left knee, she had stored this memory there, and it could have led to arthritis in later life. Through releasing this and other painful memories, her energy changed dramatically, and she took on a more positive attitude toward life.

# The Tarot Archetypes

Tarot cards are used as an aid to divination. Psychics do Tarot readings to help gain insight into present, past, and future situations; to understand the challenges and opportunities that a person is being presented with. The Tarot is very old. Some authorities believe it was used by the ancient Egyptians. It was certainly used in the fourteenth century by gypsies for fortune telling.

The cards are organized like an ordinary deck, with four suits (the Minor Arcana), plus twenty-two Trumps (the Major Arcana) and four Court cards instead of three, in a total of seventy-eight cards. Each of the cards has a symbolic picture. The Trumps have their own titles and can be seen as classic archetypes. According to psychologist Carl Jung, an archetype is derived from a racial memory present in the subconscious of each individual.

Dr. Laing instructed me to use Tarot Trumps as archetypes to illustrate the personality types that typify each chakra. He said to use the Thoth or Egyptian Tarot Deck, also known as the Crowley Deck. Each card was reproduced from an original painting by Lady Frieda Harris, under Aleister Crowley's supervision. The entire deck took her over five years to complete. This deck is remarkably universal in its scope, combining Egyptian, Greek, Christian, Hebrew and Eastern symbolism.

Some people feel uncomfortable with this deck, because Aleister Crowley was a questionable character who could best be described as an unbalanced personality with excessive energy at the sixth chakra. But he was a brilliant scholar of metaphysical symbolism. I find his own explanations of the cards pedantic and tedious, but in the end I agree with his statement that an intuitive understanding of the cards is the most valuable.

The use of the Kabbalah in this deck is especially strong. The Kabbalah is a form of Hebrew mysticism that has been called the Yoga of the West. Each Tarot Trump has a corresponding Hebrew letter. All the letters are also numbers, and they're also words. The meanings of these Hebrew words gives insight into the nature of the archetypes, so I have included them in my descriptions.

There is inherent sexism in these archetypes, but I haven't tried to avoid it, because (for example) there's a potential Emperor in every woman, and there is a potential Empress or Mother in every man.

These and other Tarot cards may be purchased at most metaphysical bookstores.

147

# Seeing Auras

Some people have the gift of literally seeing auras, the colors that surround a person. Others find they can close their eyes and feel another person's aura, and perhaps see colors with their inner vision.

Auras can be used as a form of diagnosis, since the colors that are absent from the aura indicate which colors that person requires and which chakras need energy. You can also see areas of black or brown in the aura, indicating unresolved physical or emotional traumas.

In my workshops I've found that the majority of people can feel the energy of the auras, and most people can see colors with their inner vision. The following is a simple exercise for feeling auras. In attempting this exercise, if you detect dark areas, describe their exact location to the person you're working on and they'll probably tell you about physical injuries or emotional traumas associated with those areas.

1. Stand facing your partner, about two feet away from each other.

2. Briskly rub your hands together, occasionally blowing on them.

3. Close your eyes. Hold your hands with your palms facing each other, about 8 inches apart. Feel the energy radiating between your hands. Play with this energy. Form it into a ball. Feel it growing and expanding. When the ball is about four feet in diameter, set it down.

4. Turn your palms toward your partner. Don't open your eyes. Direct the energy from your hands toward your partner.

5. Feel the energy coming from your partner's hands. Meet it with your own hands. As you do this, you'll probably find that your hands will touch your partner's hands.

6. Draw back your hands and extend your fingertips. Direct your energy through your fingertips toward your partner. Feel the energy coming from your partner's fingertips. Meet it with your own. You'll probably find that your fingertips will touch your partner's fingertips.

7. Draw back your hands and extend your index fingers. Direct your energy through your index fingers toward your partner. Feel the energy coming from your partner's index fingers. Meet it with your own. You may find that your index fingers will touch your partner's index fingers.

8. Now your partner drops his or her hands altogether. During this part of the exercise, each of you can have your eyes open or closed. Bring your hands above the top of your partner's head and attempt to feel and see the energy. Gradually work down along both sides of the head, neck, shoulders, arms, pelvis, legs, and feet, observing the energy, heat, and color that you perceive.

Then repeat the process, describing what you perceive as you move through the auras.

# Kundalini

In Hindu philosophy the goal of human life is to open all the chakras. This is known as the rising of the kundalini. Kundalini is depicted as a goddess in the form of a coiled serpent, sleeping at the base of the spine.

The goal of yoga is to awaken the kundalini to rise up the spine, awakening each chakra until she reaches the crown. There are three currents or nadis which flow in and around the spinal column like serpents spiraling around the caduceus (the familiar symbol used by the American Medical Association). The current on the left is ida, the feminine force of passion and emotion. The current on the right is pingala, the masculine force of the intellect.

When you inhale, energy moves up the ida, and when you exhale, energy moves down the pingala. Through deep concentration on the breath and developing the will power, Yoga teaches the student to bring the breath to the central channel, sushumna, which goes through the center of the spine. Then the kundalini is aroused and rises through the chakras to the highest centers, where it triggers the pineal and pituitary glands, causing a rush of energy and a brilliant experience of cosmic consciousness often described as seeing the Pure White Light and having a sense of total identity with All That Is.

This can be a glorious experience of Samadhi (Enlightenment) for one who has been well prepared through spiritual discipline: learning grounding and self control (first chakra); releasing and cleansing the emotions (second chakra), letting go of fear (third chakra) and possessiveness (fourth), and opening to one's spirituality (fifth). This is a long journey that is usually undertaken through developing a relationship with another human being who has had this experience and can guide one through the relatively unchartered waters of the sixth and seventh chakras.

Preparation is essential. Otherwise it's like introducing a high voltage electrical current into an inadequate wiring system. You may blow your fuses. One yogi (who was well prepared) reacted to his Samadhi by leaping up and running twenty-five miles. That was his way of coping with the phenomenal amount of energy that coursed through his body.

You can prepare for the kundalini to rise, but you can't control when it's going to happen. It's like the labor before childbirth: there are recognizable symptoms and many warnings, but it's a physiological phenomenon that comes in its own time—not necessarily when you want it to.

There are many possible symptoms of kundalini rising. Some are pleasant and others are extremely uncomfortable. Most of the latter are caused by resistance or lack of preparation. Symptoms include waves of heat or cold, hot flashes occurring along the acupuncture meridians, tension or pain at the sixth or seventh chakras, pain in the spine, orgasmic energy in the spine and at various parts of the body, involuntary movements of the body, spontaneous ability to do pranayama and hatha yoga (breathing and stretching exercises), unsolicited past-life flashbacks, erotic dreams, hearing voices or high-pitched sounds, and the ability to do unusual things (powers or siddhis). There may be severe emotional upsets and irrational ups and downs accompanied by copious weeping.

In fact, kundalini rising may appear very much like paranoia or psychosis. The difference is that you can usually cope by either concentrating on the external world (if that's what you need to do) or by withdrawing and going deep into meditation, where eventually (if you're fortunate) you'll break through your resistance and experience Samadhi.

If you are having some of these symptoms, try to relax and let it happen since resistance is a major cause of discomfort. If the timing isn't right or if you don't feel ready, place a carnelian at your third eye and/or two carnelian stones at your groin points. This will temporarily close down the higher chakras and pull the kundalini back down into the base chakra.

Be careful not to force Kundalini into rising prematurely. Do *not* try to visualize the serpent rising through the chakras. She will come in her own time: she prefers to be aroused when you concentrate on magnetizing your crown chakra and developing your higher self through spiritual practices.

There are always those who try to take shortcuts to enlightenment. It happens on occasion that people who've taken LSD or some other drug may inadvertently throw the switch and release the goddess Kundalini.

Whatever chakras remain undeveloped before Kundalini rises will come to haunt these people. If they're not well-grounded (first chakra), they'll feel like they're going crazy. If they didn't master their desires (second chakra), they may become hysterical or given to uncontrollable epileptic-like spasms. If they didn't master their will power (third chakra), they may force themselves upon others. If they didn't develop compassion (fourth chakra), they may become ruthless and self-serving. If they didn't develop their spirituality (the higher chakras), they may be totally disoriented, with no way to comprehend or interpret the experience.

I don't mention these things to frighten you but to explain what is meant by a premature rising of the kundalini. A study of the chakras can be a wonderful tool, but its power should not be underestimated.

If you're seeking spiritual enlightenment, if you hope to experience the rising of the kundalini, try to find a spiritual teacher; someone you trust who has had this experience and can guide you through it. It's similar to giving birth: you can have a baby all by yourself, but it's a lot nicer to have a mid-wife with you—someone who's been through it and knows what to expect.

# *Karma*

The concept of Karma is central to all Eastern religions, and it shouldn't be foreign to westerners, because it is the ultimate expression of the concept, "Do unto others as you would have others do unto you."

Karma is the belief that whatever energy and actions you exhibit will eventually return to you—like a boomerang. In some cases, the effect will be immediate, and in other cases it may take lifetimes to catch up with you.

We only use a fraction of our brain power. When Kundalini rises, she awakens dormant cells in the brain, including those that hold the memory of past lives.

I've led many clients through past lives, and it has convinced me that Karma is a reality. Whenever someone experiences inexplicable physical or emotional difficulties—especially in early life—it's easy to trace their problems back into past lives in which they created similar problems for other people.

When you believe in Karma, then rules about right and wrong are no longer necessary. There is nothing that can work more powerfully to prevent human injustice than the belief that any unkind deed that you do will be countered by an unkindness toward you—whether or not anyone else is aware of the unkindness that you have committed.

And so, when Kundalini rises, no matter how successfully we may have covered up our past—in this lifetime and others—it comes to haunt us, and we are reminded unmercifully of every misdeed that we have ever done.

The ultimate challenge, then, as Kundalini burns through our resistance, is to give unconditional love and acceptance to ourselves. Because when we learn to accept every aspect of ourselves then we are able to identify with the lowliest beggar and thief, and that is when we become truly Christ-like and utterly compassionate.

# Recommended Reading

## On Atlantis

Edgar Evans Cayce, *Edgar Cayce on Atlantis* (Warner Books, 1968).
Ruth Montgomery, *The World Before* (Fawcett Crest, 1976).

## On Crystals

Christa Faye Burka, *Clearing Crystal Consciousness* (Brotherhood of Life, 1985).
Daya Sarai Chocron, *Healing with Crystals and Gemstones* (Samuel Weiser, 1987).
Korra Deaver, Ph.D., *Rock Crystal, The Magic Stone* (Samuel Weiser, 1986).
George Frederick Kunz, *The Curious Lore of Precious Stones* (Dover Publications, 1941).
Katrina Raphaell, *Crystal Enlightenment* (Aurora Press, 1986).
Katrina Raphaell, *Crystal Healing* (Aurora Press, 1987).
Wally Richardson and Lenora Huett, *Spiritual Value of Gemstones* (DeVorss, 1983).
Uma Silbey, *The Complete Crystal Guidebook* (Bantam Books, 1987).

## On the Chakras and Yoga

Elisabeth Haich, *Sexual Energy and Yoga* (Aurora Press, 1972).
Paramahansa Yogananda, *Autobiography of a Yogi* (Self-Realization Fellowship, 1979).
Swami Sivananda Radha, *Kundalini Yoga for the West* (Timeless Books, 1978).

## On Color

Mary Anderson, *Colour Healing* (The Aquarian Press, 1983).
Alex Jones, *Seven Mansions of Color* (DeVorss & Co., 1982).
John Ott, *Health and Light*, Pocket Books, 1976).

## On the Kabbalah

Dion Fortune, *The Mystical Qabalah* (Alta Gaia, 1979).

### On Kirlian Photography

Sheila Ostrander and Lynn Schroeder, *Psychic Discoveries Behind the Iron Curtain* (Bantam Books, 1971).

### On Kundalini

Gopi Krishna, *Kundalini, The Evolutionary Energy in Man* (Shambhala, 1971).
Agit Mookerjee, *Kundalini, The Arousal of the Inner Energy* (Destiny Books, 1983).
Lee Sannella M.D., *The Kundalini Experience—Psychosis or Transcendence?* (Integral Publishing, 1987).

### On Spirit Guides

Laeh Maggie Garfield and Jack Grant, *Companions in Spirit*, (Celestial, 1984).

### On Tantra

Mantak Chia and Maneewan Chia, *Healing Love Throuth the Tao, Cultivating Female Sexual Energy* (Healing Tao Books, 1986).
Mantak Chia and Michael Winn, *Taoist Secrets of Love, Cultivating Male Sexual Energy* (Aurora Press, 1984).
Nik Douglas and Penny Slinger, *Sexual Secrets, The Alchemy of Ecstasy* (Destiny Books, 1979).

### On the Tarot

James Wanless, *New Age Tarot, Guide to the Thoth Deck* (Merrill-West, 1986).

### On Toning

Laeh Maggie Garfield, *Sound Medicine* (Celestial Arts, 1987).
Laurel Elizabeth Keyes, *Toning, The Creative Power of the Voice* (DeVorss, 1984).

### On the Yuga Cycles

Swami Sri Yukteswar, *The Holy Science* (Self-Realization Fellowship, 1977).

# References

Mary Anderson, *Colour Healing* (The Aquarian Press, 1983).

Vicki and Randall Baer, *The Crystal Connection* (Harper & Row, 1986).

Crista Faye Burka, *Clearing Crystal Consciousness* (Brotherhood of Life, 1985).

Edgar Evans Cayce, *Edgar Cayce on Atlantis* (Warner Books, 1968).

Mantak Chia and Maneewan Chia, *Healing Love Throuth the Tao, Cultivating Female Sexual Energy* (Healing Tao Books, 1986).

Mantak Chia and Michael Winn, *Taoist Secrets of Love, Cultivating Male Sexual Energy* (Aurora Press, 1984).

Aleister Crowley, *The Book of Thoth (Egyptian Tarot)* (U.S. Games Systems, Inc., 1982).

Korra Deaver, Ph.D., *Rock Crystal, The Magic Stone* (Samuel Weiser, 1986).

Dion Fortune, *The Mystical Qabalah* (Alta Gaia, 1979).

Laeh Maggie Garfield and Jack Grant, *Companions in Spirit*, (Celestial, 1984).

Elisabeth Haich, *Sexual Energy and Yoga* (Aurora Press, 1972).

Health Research, *Color Healing, An Exhaustive Survey Compiled By Health Research from the 21 Works of the Leading Practitioners of Chromotherapy* (Health Research, 1956).

Alex Jones, *Seven Mansions of Color* (DeVorss & Company, 1982).

C.W. Leadbeater, *The Chakras* (Quest, 1977).

Julia Lorusso and Joel Blick, *"Healing Stoned," The Therapeutic Use of Gems and Minerals* (Brotherhood of Life, 1983).

Dorothee L. Melia, *Stone Power* (Domel, Inc., 1979).

Ruth Montgomery, *The World Before* (Fawcett Crest, 1976).

Sheila Ostrander and Lynn Schroeder, *Psychic Discoveries Behind the Iron Curtain* (Bantam Books, 1971).

Swami Sivananda Radha, *Kundalini Yoga for the West* (Timeless Books, 1978).

Katrina Raphaell, *Crystal Enlightenment* (Aurora Press, 1986).

Katrina Raphaell, *Crystal Healing* (Aurora Press, 1987).

Wally Richardson and Lenora Huett, *Spiritual Value of Gemstones* (DeVorss, 1983).

James Wanless, *New Age Tarot, Guide to the Thoth Deck* (Merrill-West Publishing, 1986).

Sir John Woodroffe, *The Serpent Power* (Ganesh & Co., 1973).

Paramahansa Yogananda, *Autobiography of a Yogi* (Self-Realization Fellowship, 1979).

Swami Sri Yukteswar, *The Holy Science* (Self-Realization Fellowship, 1977).

# Index

Acupuncture 4
Adrenals 78
African 55
Agate 123
Agni Yoga 96
Air 82
Ajna Chakra 102
Akashic Records 111
Alcoholics 89
Aleph 116
Altar 118, 126, 127, 143
American Indian 50, 55, 130
Amethyst 34, 38, 91, 118, 123, 124, 143
Anahatha 81
Androgenous 107, 115
Anemia 58
Anesthetic 109
Anger 87
Antidote 37, 47, 135
Apache tears 60
Asthma 78
Atlantis 8, 154
Aura 4, 16, 34, 49
Auras 83, 148
*Autobiography of a Yogi* 6, 107
Aventurine 89, 123
Azurite 100, 138
Azurite with malachite 101

Babaji 116
Babies on the outside 33
Baby within 17, 28
Back pain 99, 133
Baer, Randall 23
Baer, Vicki 23, 24
Balance 79, 81
Baldness 118
Barnacle crystal 21
Base chakra 52
Bhakti Yoga 85
Black 133, 148
Black eyes 118
Black magic 104
Bladder 57

Bladder infections 58
Blankets 133
Blood 57, 58, 59, 136
Blood-cleansing foods 136
Blue 53, 57, 93, 98, 99, 138
Blue-green 64
Bones 88
*Book of Guidance, The* 11, 12, 53, 83, 73, 94, 134
*Book of the Hopi, The* 3
Bottleneck 93
Brain 109, 117
Breath of life 116
Breatharian 114
Breathing 78, 133
Brown 148
Burka, Chrysta Faye 15
Burns 99

Cabochon 123
Caddy, Eileen 3, 9
Cancer 88
Carnelian 37, 70, 123, 143, 151
Carpets 133
Catatonic 117
Cayce, Edgar 6
Celibacy 97, 107
Celibate 64
Celtic 8, 55
Cervical center 92
Chakra balance layout 35, 36
Chakras 3, 4, 45, 154
Channel 104
Channeling 10, 32, 142
Channeling crystal 32, 143
Charging the chakra 35, 37
Childbirth 58
Children 33
Christ 106
Christ consciousness 112
Christ Consciousness Center 102, 105
Citrine 6, 78, 123, 143
**Cleansing stones 126**
Cleansing the chakra 35, 38, 124, 126
Clear crystals 25
Clear quartz crystals 90, 123, 143

Clearing crystal consciousness 15
Clothing 133
Clown 115
Cluster 80
Colds 98
Colic 99
Color breathing 134
Color of Foods 136
Color-charged water 136
Colored light 131
Colored water 128
Colors 3, 47, 154
Compassion 82
Compassionate 153
Computer 110
Conditional love 86
Constipation 65, 69
Contraindications 50
Cosmic consciousness 107
Craters 26
Crowley, Aleister 147
Crown chakra 113
Crystal 123
Crystal bag 19
Crystal balancing 38
Crystal balancing and toning 35, 145
Crystal ball 5, 31
Crystal clusters 21
Crystal connection, The 23
Crystal energization 34, 35
Crystal enlightenment 10
Crystal healing 10, 33
Crystal layouts 34
Crystals 3, 154

Daleth 84
Dandruff 118
Day of rest 114
Death 114, 115, 116
Death watch 99
Debilitated 58
Decor 133
Decorations 134
Depression 117, 118
Desire 64, 65
Diabetes 78
Diana 105
Diaphragm 78
Diarrhea 65, 109
Digestion 58, 78
Digestive difficulties 78
Digestive irritation 99
Digestive organs 78

Distant healing 135
Dorsal center 81
Double terminated 19, 37, 39
Drapes 133
Drink 136
Drugs 76
Duality 102
Duodenum 78

Ear infections 99
Ears 98, 109
Earth 53
Eastern priesthoods vii
Eastern religions 153
Ego 114
Egypt 8
Egyptian Tarot Deck 147
Electro-magnetic field 15
Emotional purger 79
Emotions 101
Emperor 147
Empress 84, 147
Endocrine glands 50
Energy 69
Erotic atmosphere 133
Essene Christian 107
Excessive energy 38
Exercise 142
Exhausted 99
Exhaustion 78
Eyes 100, 109, 138

Fabric 133
Face 138
Fasting 74
Fatigue 87
Female reproductive organs 69, 84
Fertility 59
Fever 57, 99
Fire wheel 71
Float 28
Fluorite 110, 123, 143
Fluorite cluster 110
Fluorite octahedron 110
Food 136
Food allergies 78
Fool 48, 115
Fourth chakra people 83
Frigidity 58
Future 31

Gall bladder 78, 136
Gallstones 78

Garfield, Laeh 88, 89
Garnet 58, 111, 143
Gas 78
Gem 123
German glass 4, 131
German lead crystals 124
Gestalt 12
Gimel 106
Glands 50
Glass 131
Gold 106
Green 82, 138
Green quartz 89
Grey 133
Group crystal 21
Group gathering 31, 127
Guidance 9, 32, 104, 107, 144
Gum inflammation 99
Gums 138
Guru 104

Harmonic Convergence 93
Harvesting crystals 128
Hatha Yoga 55
Healing Yourself 9
Health 142
Heart 87
Heart attack 87
Heart center 81
Heart pain 87
Hebrew 8
Hebrew mysticism 147
Hemorrhoids 99
Herkimer diamonds 22
Hermit 54
Hierophant 95
High blood pressure 57, 87, 99
High-pitched tone 23
Higher intuition 104
Higher self 104, 105
Himmler, Heinrich 108
Hindu 8
Hitler 108
Hot 99
Huett, Lenora 10
Human-made gemstones 124
Humanitarian 82
Huntress 105
Hyperactive 57, 99, 118
Hyperactive children 95
Hyperthyroid 99
Hypoglycemia 78

Hypothyroid 78

Ida 102, 150
Illnesses 50
Imbalanced 49
Immortality 115, 116
Immune system 87
Impotence 58
In and out crystal 29
Incense 143
Indigo 64, 103, 109, 138
Inferiority complex 76
Infertility 58
Inflammations 57, 99, 100
Insomnia 87
Instincts 139
Internal organs 50
Intestines 109
Intuition 65, 139
Intuitive mind 105

Jade 88, 90, 143
Jaw 138
Jesus 105, 117
Jewel 123
Jewelry 126
Jewish 76
Joy 79
Judaism 49
Jung, Carl 3, 9, 147

Kabbalah 147, 154
Kahunas vii, 8
Karma 105, 153
Karma Yoga 76
Kidneys 69
Kirlian photography 4, 155
Kubler-Ross, Elisabeth 3, 10, 12
Kundalini 52, 54, 70, 95, 102, 150, 151, 155
Kundalini Center 52

Lahiri Mahasaya 116
Laing, Dr. 10, 11, 12, 46, 47, 49, 73, 74, 83, 94,
   109, 130, 138, 147
Lamp 131
Landscape 134
Lapis 109, 143
Laser 23
Light box 128, 131
Light bulb 132
Linga 52, 102
Lingam 107

Lips 138
Liver 59, 136
Liver cleansing 126
Liver problems 78
Long thin delicate crystals 25
Lotus 113
Lotus petals 46
Lovers 65
Low back pains 59
Low blood pressure 58
Lower chakra stones 126
LSD 151
Lumbar center 71
Lungs 87
Luvulite 111
Lymph glands 87, 136

Magical powers 104
Magician 106
Magnetic energies 15, 34
Mahayana Buddhism 85
Malachite 79, 124
Male reproductive organs 57, 84
Mammary glands 69
Manic-depressive 117
Manifestation 53
Manipuraka 71
Mantak Chia 143
Masks 105
Massage 31
Massage oil 79
Masseuse 133
Mayan 8
Meditation vii, 142
Meditation for peace 127
Meditation ritual 142
Medulla oblongata 103
Menopause 58, 59
Menstrual cramps 59, 101
Menstrual period 58
Mercury 107
Microcosmic Orbit 143
Midwives 83, 94
Migraine headaches 111, 117, 118
Mine 129
Miracle worker 106
Miraculous healings 115
Montgomery, Ruth 6
Mother 84, 147
Motion sickness 80
Mouth 138
Muladhara 52
Multi-terminated crystals 20

Muscle contractions 98
Muscle cramps 69, 78
Muscles 98

Nadis 150
Nature 134
Nausea 80
Navel 71
Neck 92
Negative ions 16
Negativity 87
Nerves 98
Nervous system 57, 117
Nervousness 99, 118
New age gurus 104
New age movement 84
North 34
Nose 109, 138
Note 47

Obsidian 59, 126
Occult 104
OM 103
Orange 49, 64, 95, 98, 103, 138
Organs 50
Overtired 99

Pain 31, 109
Paint 133
Pan 115
Pancreas 78
Paralysis 98
Paramahansa Yogananda 73, 107
Paranoia 151
Parasites 118
Past 31
Past lives 118, 153
Pentecostal 67
Periods 59
Perls, Fritz 3
Petals 102
Phaigh, Bethal 10, 12
Pineal 109, 117, 150
Pineal gland 105
Pingala 102, 150
Pink 82
Pink light 135
Pituitary 109, 117, 150
Plastic 131
Poor circulation 98
Pope 95
Possessive 90
Posture 143

Power 74, 78, 104, 110, 151
Power objects 143
Prana 116
Precious 123
Premenstrual cramps 59
Priestess 95, 105, 115
Private worship 96
Protection 90, 119
Protector 118
Psychic exhaustion 109
Psychic powers 104
Psychic work 100
Psychologists 5
Psychology 3
Psychosis 117, 151
Purple 118

Quaker 96
Quartz 123

Rainbows 25
Raising the dead 115
Raja Yoga 107
Rajneesh 67
Raphaell, Katrina 10, 15, 80, 110
Rashes 99
Red 53, 57, 93, 99, 138
Red face 57
Red garnet 123
Reich, Wilhelm 3
Reichi 12
Relaxation 74
Religious upbringing 98
Resh 75
Rock 123
Rock shop 124
Root chakra 52
Rose quartz 6, 89, 90, 123

Sacral center 63
Sahasrara 113
Samadhi 113, 115, 150, 151
Satir, Virginia 3
Schizophrenic 108
Self defense 135
Self confidence 70
Self realization vii, 12, 104, 105, 113
Seven 32
Sexual center 65
Sexual energy 49, 54, 57
Sexuality 50
Shamanism 3, 50, 54
Shock 58

Siddhis 151
Silica 15
Silicon dioxide 123
Silver cord 115
Single terminated 18, 36, 145
Size of stones 124
Skeptics 89
Skin 58, 69, 78
Skin irritations 99
Smell 53
Smoky quartz 38, 60, 123
Smudge 127
Snake 52, 95, 103
Sodalite 99, 143
Solar plexus 71
Sound 3
Source of All Knowledge 107
Spasms 151
Spider Woman 106
Spine 57, 143
Spirit guide 10
Spirit guides 10, 155
Spiritual teacher 104, 151
Spiritualist Church 96
Spleen 60, 63
Splenic chakra 63
Spiritual value of gemstones 10
Sri Yukteswar 6, 116
Stained glass 132
Statements 48
Stomach 78
Stone 123
Sufi 85
Sugilite 111
Superiority complex 76
Sushumna 150
Svadisthana 63
Swami Tayumanavar 12, 46
Swami Ty 12, 30
Swellings 57, 100
Swollen glands 88

Tantra 155
Tantric 97
Taoist 107
Tara 11
Tarot 3, 147, 155
Tarot Archetype 48
Teacher vii, 95
Technological 110
Teeth 88
Teething 99
Tension 87

Termination 123
Testes 57
Tharavada Buddhism 76
Third chakra people 83
Third eye 99, 103, 104, 105
Third eye center 102
Thoth 147
Thousand-petaled lotus 113
Three 32
Throat 98, 99, 138
Throat Center 92
Thymus gland 87
Thyroid 98
Tibetan 8
Tiger's Eye 69, 123
Tinctures 123, 128
Tone 38, 47, 135, 143
Tongue 138, 143
Toning 4, 11, 24, 35, 145, 155
Toning crystal 34, 36, 39, 145
Toning crystals 24
Tooled stones 124
Tooth problems 88
Toxemia 99
Toxins 136
Translucent 123
Transmutation 118
Transmute all negativity 118
Tumbled 123
Turquoise 6, 79
Tzaddi 74

Ulcers 57, 99
Unconditional love 153
Underwear 133
Unity 85

Vagina 57
Vaginal infections 99
Vajrayana Buddhist 107
Vav 95
Veils 25
Venus 84
Violet 72, 109, 113, 118, 138
Visshudha 92
Visualization 118, 134
Voice box 100
Vulnerability 90
Vulnerable 82, 89, 91

Wall Crystal 29, 34
Watermelon Tourmaline 90, 123
Waters, Frank 3

Wheezing 78
White magic 104
Who loves too much 87
Wisdom 79, 88
Wisdom chakra 113
Witch hazel 79
Womb stones 60
Women's intuition 65
Workaholic 76

Yellow 49, 72, 98, 138
Yod 55
Yoga 154
Yogananda 6, 116
Yogis 4
Yoni 102
Yuga 93
Yuga cycles 155

Zain 66

# Explanation of Back Cover

The colored cloths are arranged in progressively larger sizes as you proceed upward. Each color represents one of the seven chakras. According to Dr. Laing, "In a highly evolved person, the chakras are like progressively larger fountains, with the yellow of personal power tumbling over the orange of sexuality, which is brimming over the small but brilliant red of a firm foundation."

1. garnet in matrix
2. garnet mounted on crystal
3. smoky quartz points
4. obsidian spears
5. apache tears (obsidian)
6. carnelianized petrified wood
7. carnelian cabochon
8. rough carnelian
9. tiger's eye
10. malachite eggs
11. malachite cabochon
12. tumbled citrine
13. citrine crystal
14. turquoise cabochons
15. rough turquoise
16. rough rose quartz
17. tumbled rose quartz
18. cut watermelon tourmaline
19. watermelon tourmaline pieces
20. tumbled aventurine
21. polished aventurine
22. polished B.C. jade
23. water-worn B.C. jade
24. water-worn Monterey jade
25. rough azurite
26. azurite cabochon
27. sodalite cabochon
28. rough sodalite
29. polished lapis
30. lapis cabochon
31. rough lapis
32. sugilite
33. fluorite octahedrons
34. fluorite clusters
35. clear quartz clusters
36. long toning crystal
    (single terminated)
37. single terminated crystal
38. channeling crystal
39. long thin delicate crystals
40. Herkimer diamond
41. crystal ball
42. double terminated crystal
43. tumbled amethyst
44. amethyst point
45. amethyst cluster

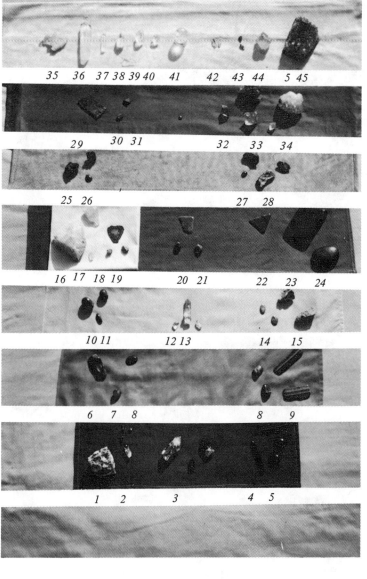

# OTHER RELATED BOOKS BY THE CROSSING PRESS

*Ariadne's Thread: A Workbook of Goddess Magic*
**By Shekhinah Mountainwater**
"One of the finest books on women's spirituality available."
—Sagewoman
**$14.95 • Paper • 0-89594-475-8**

*An Astrological Herbal for Women*
**By Elisabeth Brooke**
An extensive guide to the use of herbs in healing the mind, body, and spirit, organized by planetary influence. Brooke describes the mythological history and astrological significance of 38 common herbs, as well as their physical, emotional and ritual uses. Herbal recipes for food and medicine are also provided.
**$12.95 • Paper • 0-89594-740-4**

*The Healing Energy of Your Hands*
**By Michael Bradford**
The techniques described are so simple that anyone, even a child, can begin to sense and work with healing energy.
**$12.95 • Paper • 0-89594-781-1**

*The Healing Voice: Traditional & Contemporary Toning,*
*Chanting and Singing*
**By Joy Gardner Gordon**
"In a fascinating blend of comparative anthropology, spiritual autobiography, and how-to, Gardner-Gordon asserts that most religious traditions have recognized the spiritual and biomedical efficacy of chanting and other forms of "toning" but acknowledges as well that Judeo-Christian culture slights this powerful means of contact between mind and body and between mind-body and the divine."
—Booklist
**$12.95 • Paper • 0-89594-571-1**

*Mother Wit: A Guide to Healing and Psychic Development*
**By Diane Mariechild**
"One of the most nurturing feminine-wise books available today for developing our inherent psychic abilities."
—Womanspirit Sourcebook
Over 150,000 in Print
**$12.95 • Paper • 0-89594-358-1**

*The Sevenfold Journey:*
*Reclaiming Mind, Body and Spirit Through the Chakras*
**By Anodea Judith and Selene Vega**

"If you do the work this book suggests, changes will happen in your life, no matter what belief system you subscribe to. Judith and Vega may well have written a classic." —Gnosis
**$18.95 • Paper • 0-89594-574-6**

*The Wiccan Path: A Guide to the Solitary Practitioner*
**By Rae Beth**

A modern guide to the ancient path of the village wisewoman. Writing in the form of letters to her two apprentices, Rae Beth provides rituals for all the key festivals of the wiccan calendar, describes the therapeutic powers of trancework and herbalism, and outlines the Pagan approach to finding a partner.
**$12.95 • Paper • 0-89594-744-7**

*A Wisewoman's Guide to Spells, Rituals, and Goddess Lore*
**By Elisabeth Brooke**

Gathering together for the very first time all the disciplines of European witchcraft and giving rituals and spells for us to use, this is a remarkable compendium of magical lore, psychic skills and women's mysteries.
**$12.95 • Paper • 0-89594-779-X**

✳

*Please look for these books*
*at your local bookstore or order from*
**The Crossing Press**
**P.O. Box 1048, Freedom, CA 95019.**

*Add $2.50 for the first book and 50¢ for each*
*additional book. Or call toll free 800-777-1048*
*with your credit card order.*